BIBLICAL
COUNSELING
WITH
AFRICAN-
AMERICANS

BIBLICAL COUNSELING
WITH
AFRICAN-AMERICANS

Taking a Ride in the Ethiopian's Chariot

CLARENCE WALKER

ZondervanPublishingHouse

Grand Rapids, Michigan

A Division of HarperCollinsPublishers

Biblical Counseling With African-Americans
Copyright © 1992 by Clarence Walker

Requests for information should be addressed to:
Zondervan Publishing House
Grand Rapids, Michigan 49530

Library of Congress Cataloging-in-Publication Data

Walker, Clarence.
    Biblical counseling with African-Americans : taking a ride in the Ethiopian's chariot / Clarence Walker.
        p.   cm.
    Includes bibliographical references.
    ISBN 0-310-58711-5
    1. Afro-Americans—Pastoral counseling of. 2. Afro-Americans—Psychology. I. Title.
    BV4468.2.A34W35   1992   92-16146
    253.5′08996073—dc20   CIP

Unless otherwise noted, all Scripture quotations are taken from the King James Version of the Holy Bible.

Edited by Harriet Crosby
Cover design by the Aslan Group

Printed in the United States of America

95 96 97 98 99 00 01 02 /❖ DH / 9 8 7 6 5 4 3

CONTENTS

Discerning How Black Counselees Get Stuck
Selecting Intervention Starting Points

INTRODUCTION

The subtitle of this book is based on the biblical account of the disciple Philip's encounter with an Ethiopian eunuch recorded in Acts 8:26–39. Traditionally, this passage has been seen as a soul-winning effort on the part of Philip to a black man from Ethiopia. However, I suggest that this story involves more than evangelism; it is a wonderful illustration of Bible-based counseling as it relates to black counselees.

The purpose of this book is to set forth the issues, principles, and interventions of counseling as revealed by the Holy Spirit through God's Word, and apply them in the counseling of African-Americans, especially in terms of marriage counseling and family therapy. To demonstrate this, I will draw upon my own experience as a marriage counselor and ordained minister in private practice in Philadelphia. The major points will be discussed in light of Acts 8:26–39, and elaborated throughout the course of the book.

As I expound these points, I do so with some underlying assumptions. First, successful biblical counseling with black counselees should have three integrated components as part of its framework. It should be based on a sound biblical foundation; incorporate both Christian and secular theory where consistent with Scripture; and it should be relevant to the unique ethnic characteristics peculiar to black people.

I also assume that ethnicity plays a role in the context of therapy which black and white counselors must respect.

The third assumption I make is that the clinical case experience is a viable research methodology, one often overlooked and underutilized in the mental health disciplines. Moreover, while the clinical-case approach lacks the methodological rigor of statistical testing, instruments, control groups, and the like, it adds a missing factor. It affords clinicians and clergy the opportunity to develop a relationship with people and observe their behavior in a way impossible for a researcher absorbed in statistics and correlations.

Finally, I assume that the Holy Spirit, as God's primary enabling agent, may empower anyone—black or white—to counsel black counselees. Therefore, the Holy Spirit leading in conjunction with the Scriptures takes priority over human wisdom. These assumptions are foundational to the concepts in this book.

Biblical Counseling With African-Americans is divided into three parts. Part I, Counseling Issues With Black Counselees, addresses seven issues that often arise in the context of counseling. These issues stem from important information concerning the Ethiopian eunuch found in Acts 8:27. We are given data regarding their ethnicity, gender, sexuality, power status, socio-economic level, environment, and religion. These are the same issues counselors face in counseling black people. We shall closely examine these issues in terms of their implications, indications (certain intervention should be employed), and contra-indications (intervention should not be employed) for counseling.

Part II, The Counseling Process and Black Counselees: Ten Biblical Principles, discusses ten principles counselors should follow in developing an effective therapeutic process. These principles are derived from Acts 8:26–39 and were used by Philip in his encounter with the eunuch.

Part III, Therapeutic Interventions, demonstrates the use of biblical techniques for treatment with couples and individuals.

The Holy Spirit enabled Philip to touch a black man and in a significant way. The same Holy Spirit can empower counselors to reach black people for Christ through biblical counseling. The balance of this book presents Scripture and a process that equips counselors to ride in the Ethiopian's chariot.

Part I

COUNSELING ISSUES WITH BLACK COUNSELEES

1

ETHNICITY ISSUES

"A Man of Ethiopia" (Acts 8:27)

One of the first challenges faced by Philip in Acts 8:27 was the fact that the eunuch was an Ethiopian, a man of a different ethnicity and nationality. This same issue confronts the non-black counselor seeking a therapeutic relationship with black counselees. If counselors are to experience a successful chariot ride through the course of counseling, it is important that they recognize the possible impact of ethnicity. When this factor is not taken into consideration, it may lead to mistaken presumptions concerning behavior observed in counseling. Often blacks are viewed through ethnocentric glasses and evaluated by white middle-class norms.

On the other hand, counselors can be influenced by ethnicity in stereotyping African-Americans as a people. This notion is just as counterproductive as the view that depreciates the importance of racial factors. Counselors need to be aware of these factors without attaching too much significance to either of them. They should maintain a balanced view. Counselors, whether clinicians or clergy, must be cognizant of their own values about African-Americans and how they may negatively influence the therapeutic alliance. As a general Christian ethic, we ought to operate on the following premises: "God is no respecter of persons: But in every nation he that feareth him, and worketh righteousness, is accepted with him" (Acts 10:34–35); in Christ "there is neither Jew nor Greek" (Galatians 3:28) and God "hath made of one blood all nations of men for to dwell on all the face of the earth" (Acts 17:26).

Even so, the question still remains: what is the role of black ethnicity in therapy? Since most counselors, Christian or otherwise, have had little knowledge of blacks, a good place to start is their familial kinship history from West Africa to America.

WEST AFRICAN FAMILIAL STRUCTURES

From the work of black scholars we learn that each aspect in the lives of West Africans was permeated with the African belief in strong kinship bonds. The notion of rugged individualism dominated European economic philosophy. However, the West African land was owned not by individuals, but by the tribal or familial group.[1] Various African tribes shared in the area of kinship an intra-tribal sense of collective unity and adopted the philosophy "we are; therefore I am."[2] Consequently, an individual was nobody because the self was defined in relationship to others. One was a son, a daughter, a parent, or a grandparent, and had a large or small place in the village. One was known in relationship to others and shared the reputation of kin. A wastrel or cowardly brother was one's own shame; a relation who brought glory to himself was one's own pride; and the kinsman whose name one shared carried force and qualities of others.[3] Each person was linked through family to others in the village so that, to the West African mind, the village became the family writ large.[4]

Huggins' description of the sixteenth-century family life typical of West Africans stated:

> You would have yourself centered in your mother's house with her other children, your brother and your sister. Most likely, there would be near at hand women like your mother, the wives of your father, their children, your half brothers and sisters, like yourself from your father's seed. At the core of the Universe would stand your father. There would be a senior wife who stood above the other women in authority. Then there would be the co-wives with your mother and all the children ranging in age from infancy to adulthood.[5]

In this kind of compound, the familial network of relationships extended outward to encompass uncles and aunts, cousins, nieces, and nephews. In addition, the compound often housed other individuals, slaves captured in war who worked in the family interest but were allowed to enter the family through marriage.[6]

From West African history we learn several things about kinship patterns that existed within the socio-cultural and ethnic framework of the ancestors of African-Americans.

In the first place, there was a strong sense of family. It was a force so powerful that one's personal identity was determined by it. Second, this familial identity was intergenerational and multigenerational. Third, the black male occupied a prominent role in the family, which carried the veneration of spouse and offspring. This, then, was the socio-cultural orientation that the people of West Africa brought with them on slave ships to America.

Notwithstanding, a controversial question still remains: did the descendants of West Africans brought to the United States continue the kinship patterns under which their predecessors were socialized? There is evidence that vestiges of West African culture remained part of the social fabric of blacks in America.

BLACK FAMILY KINSHIP PATTERNS

The belief that residues of West African culture survived and remained part of the cultural scheme of blacks is referred to as the Africanity theory. There is credibility to this theory based on evidence of afroisms found among the blacks of North America, the Caribbean, and some parts of South America. These afroisms are used in art, music, religion, and kinship relations of these regions.[7] Concerning kinship, the work of Gutman has shown that black families exhibited amazing survival resilience in the face of adverse conditions. Gutman examined documents and census data that had accumulated between 1750 and 1925 and discovered most black homes were two-parent homes and that a strong kinship network remained intact. His research refuted the myth of the matriarchal black family wherein domineering black women headed single-parent homes in the absence of black men.[8] The evidence suggests that blacks did maintain a strong sense of family kinship in spite of that peculiar institution known as slavery.

Furthermore, black families continue to sustain strong kinship bonds and intergenerational networks.[9] African-Americans are a multigenerational kinship people. It is not unusual to have two to three generations living in the same house. The grandmother in particular is a central figure in many black families and is often involved in rearing a couple of generations of children. The multigenerational kinship patterns of blacks is not merely a socio-economic adaptation. Middle-class blacks often perpetuate the same kinship designs even though they are of a different socio-economic stratum from poor blacks.[10]

To understand black families, it is important to note that most of them draw from two sources to form their familial identity: their West African roots and their American roots. In other words, one must think of the black family as West African in nature and American in nurture.[11] As a result, familial kinships often maintain six characteristics:

1. Black families may be comprised of several individual households with the family definition and lines of authority and support transcending or going beyond any one household unit that comprises the family.

2. They maintain elasticity—that is they are structurally expanding and diminishing in response to external conditions.

3. They have a child-centered system (the general organization often requires and focuses on children).

4. They often have close network relationships between families not necessarily related by blood.

5. They have flexible and interchangeable role definitions and performance.

6. They have multiple parenting and interfamilial consensual adoptions.[12]

An example of some of the features of black-family structure and network is illustrated in the following case.

John H. was a forty-five-year-old black man who had been separated from his wife for about ten years. During the separation he raised his two daughters, thirteen-year-old Sharon and twelve-year-old Maggie, both of whom were in his custody. Jean, the mother of the two girls, was thirty-two years old and lived on welfare. She was living in a household with her mother, sisters, nieces, nephews, and paramours. During Jean's stay with her mother she had borne children out of wedlock by two different fathers. Both men had stayed at the household on more than one occasion.

John and Jean were in the process of filing for divorce and were locked in court battles over custody of Sharon. A court social worker referred them to a marriage council. The presenting problem was the difficulty Sharon experienced at school in relationships and grades. She had also decided to leave her father to go stay with her mother, which upset her father greatly.

At the therapy session the following people were present: John the father; Jean the mother; Sharon; Jean's eight-year-old daughter and three-month-old infant—both born out of wedlock. In the course of therapy it was learned that Sharon stayed with her mother in her grandmother's household, but alternated on weekends and stayed with her father and sister Maggie.

The structure of this family is not uncommon among lower-income black families. It is illustrative of the characteristics previously mentioned. The identified patient was a child typical of the child-centered system that is often part of the general family organization. This family included the paramours of Sharon's mother as well as various aunts, a situation consistent with blacks often having relations with people not related by blood. There are fluid features of the multiple and transient roles Sharon experienced.

To the counselor who does not understand kinship interrelations of black-family functioning, this appears as a very dysfunctional, emeshed, and disorganized family in contrast to the biblical standard for the home. Some dysfunction is present, but there are also strengths in this family that need to be identified. The Christian counselor, while unable to condone sin in the family, must recognize its kinship strengths. Identification of kinship strengths is one of the primary means, along with the influence of the larger culture, in development of black self-concept.

BLACK SELF-CONCEPT DEVELOPMENT

The issue of black self-concept is shaped by three cultural sources: residuals from Africa; adaptations and responses to systematic victimization, a product of racism, poverty and oppression; and identification with mainstream America. Values from all three of these sources are found in black families and account for diversity in values and behavior. Generally, there are three adaptive responses that blacks often choose as coping mechanisms. They may remain isolated from American mainstream culture and identify exclusively with one's own subculture; identify exclusively with American mainstream culture; or try to integrate the two.[13] Blacks have not often been allowed the latter two options, but diagnosed as pathological for selecting the former. Consequently, African-American people are a heterogeneous group distributed from one end of the value continuum to the other.

Self-esteem is an essential part of anyone's development. But many blacks suffer from low self-esteem. James Dobson says that low self-esteem engulfs anyone who feels disrespect from other people. He also claims that at least ninety percent of our self-image is built from what we think others think about us. It is difficult for an individual to have self-respect if the rest of the world seems to believe that person is dumb or ugly or lazy, boring, uncreative or undesirable.[14] Given the legacy of treatment in America, racial minorities have often felt that the rest of the world believed these negative things about them. Thus, blacks often compartmentalize their self-esteem. Compartmentalizing enables them to accept themselves but reject their larger ethnic group, which is associated with the negative images the dominant society has of them.[15]

This kind of compartmentalizing is characteristic of many black middle-class Christians I have seen in therapy. They do not want to be identified with those other blacks that are dumb, ugly, lazy, boring, uncreative and undesirable.[16] This condescending attitude reflects a form of self-hate rampant in the black middle class and is a product of accepting personal identity over ethnical identity. Self-hate is not scriptural. In Psalm 139:14 we read that we are "fearfully and wonderfully made." Part of who God made us to be includes our ethnicity and racial heritage. To reject this aspect of our being is to reject God's creation. In light of this, Christian counselors need to enable African-Americans to identify their lack of self-esteem as well as the incongruence between their personal image and broader ethic image. And they must encourage African-Americans to develop the kind of self-love that springs from being made in God's image as a magnificent example of his creative ingenuity. Concerning self-love, Gary Collins states:

> Compared with secular perspectives of self-love, the Bible assumes that we will love ourselves. This assumption is difficult for some Christians to accept because they equate self-love with an attitude of superiority; self-love is not an erotic or ecstatic self-adoration. Self-love means to see ourselves worthwhile creatures valued and loved by God, gifted members of the body of Christ, bearers of the Divine nature.[17]

The following case example illustrates a problematic black self-concept.

> William is a thirty-six-year-old black man. His wife, Betty, is also thirty-six years old. They have been married for seven years and have two children from this union. William was a carpenter but had experienced great difficulty finding work. Betty was a bank teller who worked only part-time. Thus, the family was under severe economic stress.
>
> The presenting problem was that communication had become unbearable. The couple had a communication style based on conflict. Betty would nag William for his seeming irresponsibility and immaturity. She concluded he was not trying hard enough to get a job, and it appeared that the more she pushed him to be responsible the less responsible he became. She felt he had time for everyone but her. She had particular disdain for the amount of time and attention he gave to his mother and sisters. William, on the other hand, complained that Betty was sexually unresponsive,

cold, demanding, and domineering. After the first meeting with them, the counselor learned that Betty had been sexually molested by her step-father from the age of nine until she was thirteen. William was the only male in a family of six girls where he was pampered. He developed a passive-aggressive dependency on his wife.

The backgrounds of this couple, among other things, revealed that they both suffered from feelings of inadequacy and a lack of self-love. In an individual session with Betty it was clear that the molesting done to her left her feeling dirty, ugly, and undesirable. She cried often as she remembered feeling hurt, degraded, and worthless. She felt God was punishing her and did not love her. She felt this way in spite of the fact that she was a born-again Christian. William also showed signs of low self-esteem even though he too was a born-again believer. Recounting his frustration as a black man trying to find a job, he cried when he expressed how he had put in several applications, prayed about each one, but knew he would not get work because he was black. He stated that when he gets to heaven he is going to ask God why he had to make life so hard by cursing black people the way he did.

My work with Betty involved helping her to face some of the guilt and rage she felt, and getting her to see the scars left on her self-image from her experience of sexual abuse. After a number of sessions and by the leading of the Holy Spirit, I gently challenged some of the negative feelings she held about herself. I showed her in Scripture that she did have self-worth in God's eyes. We began to look at all of her mental, spiritual, and physical endowments. We reviewed the fact that she was a vital member of the body of Christ. She was likened to persons such as David, Jacob, and Leah who were not held in high esteem by members of their families, but who became great for God. After several sessions of this, I noticed a distinct change in her attitude about herself. She became more pleasant, amiable, and self-assured.

Work with William focused on his feelings of inferiority that underlay his passive-aggressive dependency. After about three sessions he was able to see the connection between his behavior and his feelings of inadequacy. I began working with him on his self-image, encouraging him to be more assertive and positive. I reminded him that he should not view his blackness as a handicap but rather as a gift from God. I said that in spite of his blackness, "greater is he that is in him than he that is in the world" and that "he is more than a conqueror through Christ." After several sessions, he became more positively aggressive and self-confident.

It is this self-loving attitude minority counselees must come to accept. The Christian counselor in the hand of God, is an instrument to facilitate its development.

When issues of black self-concept, multi-generational familial structures, and other Africanisms come together they have a profound impact on a counseling setting. The results of such counseling settings often distinguish black counselees from white counselees.

BLACK COUNSELEES AND WHITE COUNSELEES

Psychodynamically, there are no differences between blacks and whites. There are, however, ethnic or cultural differences that may cause black counselees to behave differently in therapy. Seven possible reactions to the therapeutic setting are:

1. African-Americans may be more unfamiliar with therapy and ignorant of the process than white counselees.

2. They often present more severe problems because they wait until a crisis.

3. They often expect and want shorter therapy.

4. They tend to disclose less about themselves than whites, and black males disclose less than black females.

5. They operate on cultural values about time and can be chronically late or not show up for appointments without notification.

6. Their presenting problem may be stress as a result of striving for upward mobility.

7. Their psychological development has been shaped by racism.[18]

Black men in particular may be obstinate in their willingness to divulge personal information. Despite this, the Holy Spirit can enable Christian counselors to work with clients' ethnicity as he did with Philip's encounter with the Ethiopian. Practitioners need to be sensitive to this issue so that they can better understand the function of ethnicity in the counseling process. And the Scriptures do tell us "with all thy getting get understanding" (Proverbs 4:7). In the final analysis, prudent clinicians and clergy remember that it is "not by might, nor by power, but by my spirit, saith the LORD of hosts" (Zechariah 4:6).

The prophet asked the question, "Can the Ethiopian change his skin?" (Jeremiah 13:23). The answer is no. God wants his ebony-skinned children to accept themselves, love themselves, and see themselves as a beautiful part of creation.

NOTES

[1]Nathan Huggins, *Black Odyssey: The Afro-American Ordeal in Slavery* (New York: Vintage Books, 1985), 1–24.

[2]Ibid.

[3]Ibid.

[4]Ibid., 14–16.

[5]Ibid., 21-22.

[6]Ibid.

[7]Ibid.

[8]Herbert Gutman, *The Black Family in Slavery and Freedom 1750–1925* (New York: Vintage Books, 1976), 461–74.

[9]Ibid.

[10]Robert Joseph Taylor, "Receipt of Support From Family Among Black and Familial Differences," *Journal of Marriage and the Family* 48 (February 1986), 67–77.

[11]Elaine Pinderhughes, "Afro-American Families and the Victim System," *Ethnicity and Family Therapy*, eds. John K. Pearch and Monica McGoldrick (Westport: Greenwood, 1983), 105–21.

[12]Ibid.

[13]Ibid.

[14]James Dobson, *What Wives Wish Their Husbands Knew About Women* (Wheaton: Tyndale, 1975), 22–57.

[15]Pinderhughes, "Afro-American Families," 165.

[16]Dobson, *What Wives Wish*, 25–51.

[17]Gary R. Collins, *Christian Counseling: A Comprehensive Guide* (Waco: Word, 1960), 349.

[18]Lorraine Brannon, "Marriage and Family Therapy With Black Clients: Methods and Structure," *Black Marriage and Family Therapy*, ed. Constance E. Obudha, (Westport: Greenwood, 1983), 174–75.

2

GENDER ISSUES

"A man of Ethiopia" (Acts 8:27)

We discover in Acts 8:27 that Philip arose and went to join this "man of Ethiopia." He not only had to deal with the issue of ethnicity regarding the eunuch, but also with the fact that he was a *man* from Ethiopia. Gender is a significant issue in therapy, affecting the efficacy of the counseling process and outcome.

For black men, the issue of masculinity has been a sensitive factor for them in America. Noted sociologist Robert Staples relates that black men face problems that do not prepare them very well for the fulfillment of their masculine roles. Therefore, they encounter negative stereotyping about themselves that exists on all levels.[1] Gender may surface as an issue in the counseling process as therapy progresses, in some cases preempting other issues. This is especially possible when exploring black men's sense of masculinity or black male/female dynamics in general.

BLACK MASCULINITY

One of the questions regarding the issue of black masculinity is: what kind of role models do black men emulate during their youth? There is the inaccurate assumption that the only models are pimps, hustlers, street-corner men, and petty criminals. This is not necessarily the case.

African-American men draw positive role examples from a

variety of sources: a hard-working grandfather, a successful athlete on television, a dedicated social worker, a respected older brother, an involved community leader, a good neighbor, and, not least, a dedicated churchman. Even though many black men may have experienced the absence of a father, they have reached into other arenas of their community to adopt virtuous role models.

Furthermore, black youth have also used white males as examples in the socialization of their masculine identity. So whites who served in the capacity of school coach, teacher, police officer, social worker, parole officer, recreational worker, or local businessman provided positive images when respectable black ones were lacking. Black male children have demonstrated a resourceful ability to expand beyond their own race in developing their gender identity. There is nothing offensive about this so long as the identification is based on gender, not race, and the youth make the distinction. The male role models on whom youth build their gender identity may come from a diversity of personalities either inside or outside of the black community. Black men have essentially taken what has been available to them.

In addition, counselors must not make the error of assuming that blacks automatically develop poor identities when reared in homes with a woman as head of household. For the most part, these female single parents have done a commendable job raising their male young in the face of seemingly impossible odds. We understand the scriptural teaching that God's order is for men to be head of their homes (Ephesians 5:23). It is important to understand that, for a plethora of reasons (such as abandonment, economics, divorce, widowhood, etc.), it is not always possible for men to head households in the black community.

African-American women have been unfairly saddled with the responsibility of dual gender roles as parents. Counselors must understand that women profoundly affect the evolution of the male identity of their sons without pejorative side effects. The Bible contains several such examples. In the case of Timothy, Paul recounts the source of Timothy's faith, stating, ". . . I call to remembrance the unfeigned faith that is in thee, which dwelt first in thy grandmother Lois, and thy mother Eunice; and I am persuaded that in thee also" (2 Timothy 1:5). Also worthy of mention is Hannah's effect on Samuel (1 Samuel 1:26–28). There are many other noteworthy women who were instrumental in shaping good images for their male offspring.

Nevertheless, if black males have not had positive role models and suffer gender insecurities, the results may mean problems in their marriages, and even prevent them from seeking therapy. They may conclude that they are something less than men for seeking counseling. In addition, black men may believe that therapy is for crazy folks. Lorraine Brannon says that one of the obstacles to black males seeking therapy is their tendency to stigmatize it as something for the weak. So they may be formidably resistant to counseling, at least initially.[2]

If a couple brings marital problems into counseling, insecurities concerning either gender or ethnicity are sure to disrupt marital harmony.

BLACK MALE AND FEMALE INTERACTIVE DYNAMICS

Black male and female interaction has been portrayed by the media primarily as one of conflict. The perception we are left with is that there is no love between the two. But is this perception accurate? Is there no love in black marriages, or do these couples define it differently than whites?[3]

Ruth King and Jean Griffin embarked upon a research project to ascertain what blacks viewed love to be. They surveyed males and females between the ages of fifteen and fifty. A seventeen-item questionnaire was used with two hundred couples. They received a sixty percent response. The group was fifty-three percent females and forty-seven percent male. Moreover, forty-six percent were married, twenty-four percent single, and twenty percent were separated or divorced. The survey revealed that blacks in the group tended to define love in terms of trust, respect, compatibility, caring, and warmth. Those who were over thirty years old regarded environmental factors as significant, while participants under thirty did not. College students tended to develop loving relationships with the opposite sex that would culminate in marriage.[4]

The study suggests that blacks do believe in love and, like whites, expect it to include certain virtues. At the same time, there does seem to be widespread discord between black males and females that contribute to the high dissolution rate of marriages. What is the origin of the estrangement between black men and women? Jill Nelson claims, "Black men fear love. They possess a fear that grows up in all those fatherless black homes that are so numerous they have come to characterize black culture."[5]

Another reason for estrangement is the anger African-American males and females have toward each other. In reality it is anger harbored toward larger society. But such anger cannot be expressed without severe social reprisal. Thus, rage is either turned on one's mate or oneself. In marriage, it is more likely to be focused on one's mate, in the form of spousal abuse, or expressed through volatile communication styles. Black psychiatrists Price Cobbs and William Grier label this anger "black rage."[6] Dr. Alvin Poussaint explains anger as the reason why blacks resort to killing other blacks.[7] Newspapers all across this country carry tragic stories of black domestic violence resulting in the maiming, injury, or murder of spouses because of angry outbursts. Consequently, Christian practitioners should help black couples address their anger from both practical and biblical perspectives. Counselors may also have to teach conflict-resolution methods and anger-reduction skills.

Male and female interaction of African-Americans frequently exhibits itself in the sexuality of the couple. Sex is a symbol of health in a couple's relationship. If there are other problems in the marriage, sex is one of the places where problems will manifest themselves. The issue of sexuality is one that requires focused attention.

NOTES

[1]Robert Staples, *Black Masculinity: The Black Male's Role in American Society* (San Francisco: Black Scholar Press, 1982), 7–8.

[2]Brannon, *Marriage and Family*, 175

[3]Ruth E. G. King and Jean T. Griffin, "The Loving Relationship: Impetus for Black Marriage," *Black Marriage And Family Therapy*, ed. Constance E. Obudha (Westport: Greenwood, 1983), 14–20.

[4]Ibid.

[5]George Davis and Jill Nelson, "Come Out With Your Hands: How Black Men and Women Really Feel About Each Other," *Essence* (July 1986): 54–56.

[6]William H. Grier and Price M. Cobbs, *Black Rage* (New York: Basic Books, 1968), 20–80.

[7]Alvin Poissant, *Why Blacks Kill Blacks* (New York: Emerson Hall, 1972), 59–80.

3

SEXUAL ISSUES

"An eunuch" (Acts 8:27)

Another fact about the man from Ethiopia is that he was a eunuch (Acts 8:27). The man's particular sexual identity involved abstinence. Whether his lack of sexual activity was due to castration or to a personal decision, the Scriptures do not make clear. Nevertheless, it was a key to his identity.

There are probably not many black men today willing to classify themselves as eunuchs, but they do have concepts of their own sexual identity. So the coital preferences, ideas, orientations, myths, and stereotypes that African-Americans bring to counseling must be given proper respect by practitioners.

SEXUALITY, SEXUAL ORIENTATIONS, AND BLACK COUNSELEES

Sexual feelings are a part of normal human functioning. It was God's idea to create this pleasurable human experience. Yet many Christians have a great deal of anxiety, fear, and apprehension about their sexuality. They harbor myths, stereotypes, and misinformation on the issue unfortunately fostered by bad teaching on the part of the church. The fact remains that we are sexual in some way. And in today's world of rapid social changes, a plurality of sexual preferences have emerged. We may be called upon to advise those in heterosexual relationships within marriage, heterosexual relationships outside of marriage, homosexual relationships, bisexual relationships, and even celibacy.

Although the Scriptures address all of these forms of sexual expression, it sanctions only two—heterosexual relations within marriage (see Genesis 2:24 and 1 Corinthians 7:1–5) and celibacy (see Matthew 19:12 and 1 Corinthians 7:7–9). All other sexual expressions are condemned—bisexuality and homosexuality (see 1 Corinthians 6:9; 1 Timothy 1:10; and Romans 1:26–27), and fornication and adultery (see 1 Corinthians 6:9, 18; Exodus 20:14; and 1 Thessalonians 4:3).

Christian counselors find that black counselees bring their sexual issues to therapy either directly as a dysfunction, or indirectly as an issue growing out of other presenting problems. Frequently, those who enter therapy because of sexual problems come with such things as an erectile dysfunction, ISD (inhibited sexual desire), premature ejaculation, preorgasmia, or vaginismus.

But the most common sexual issue for which a black couple comes to counseling is an extramarital affair on the part of the husband. Robert Staples states that sexual infidelity accounts for more than forty percent of the termination of black marriages.[1] Marriages of black men are often disrupted by the "other woman" because competition among black women for the low supply of educated black males is keen. This is a predicament for single black women who already outnumber their men by 1.4 million. They recognize that the most desirable black males are already married. Many single women seek married men to fulfill their longings for male companionship. Ironically, as long as they continue financial support, many married black women resign themselves to their husbands' infidelity. The following case example illustrates this point.

Lewis and Adrian made an appointment for marital counseling. Lewis was a forty-five-year-old black man employed by the local telephone company as a lineman. Adrian, a thirty-eight-year-old black woman, was a homemaker. They had been married for seven years and had one five-year-old son. Adrian had another daughter by a previous marriage.

The presenting problem was the volatile arguments the couple had been having for the last year, which ended with Adrian securing a gun and threatening her husband's life. Adrian complained that Lewis was aloof, did not communicate with the family, worked too much and came home at strange hours. Lewis complained that Adrian did not keep the house clean and did not trust him. Through discerning the Holy Spirit, I sensed that the husband was having an affair, which was a major factor in the couple's marital troubles. At the end of the session, Adrian claimed that Lewis had had an affair. Lewis denied this and said that the woman in question was just a friend from the job with whom he occasionally had lunch. I took note of the issue of the affair but did not pursue it at the first session. I knew that pursuing the issue too soon would drive the male out of therapy and destroy any chance of successful work as a couple.

The couple contracted for a second session on Wednesday of the following week, but Adrian called on Monday to indicate that the session would have to be canceled. The couple had another argument and Lewis left to go with the other woman with whom he earlier denied having an affair. Adrian agreed to continue individual therapy.

At the second session, Adrian was clearly not upset that her husband was with another woman. I questioned her about this. She responded that she could not understand why she was not more outraged and angered, but her greatest concern was how she would support herself and her children. Adrian stated that she had resigned herself to the fact that this is how black men are.

A week later Lewis was thrown out by the other woman. He promptly called Adrian who went over to the other woman's house and helped Lewis move his things back home. She did this without reservation and showed no sign of anger at the fact that he had an affair.

There are obviously other pyschodynamics at work with this couple that go beyond the issue of the affair. But it demonstrates the stance many black women take in coping with their husbands' unfaithfulness. To them it is a case of black men being black men.

A heterosexual orientation may not be the only sexual issue brought to therapy. A counselee may come with feelings of guilt regarding homosexuality or bisexuality. There are a number of black individuals who enter counseling with these latent or overt tendencies.

The compilation of statistics concerning the AIDS epidemic bears evidence that the dreaded disease is taking its toll on blacks. According to Dr. Rudolph E. Jackson, a medical consultant with the Centers for Disease Control in Atlanta, blacks comprise twenty-five percent of those diagnosed with AIDS, fifty percent of heterosexual cases reported and fifty-one percent of female cases. Sixty-six percent of all AIDS patients are homosexuals. Of the black AIDS victims, thirty-two percent are homosexual or bisexual.[2] These percentages indicate the existence of an active homosexual and bisexual population within the black community.

There is a good possibility that at some point Christian counselors will deal with individuals or couples with varying degrees of homosexual or bisexual inclinations. Black homosexuals face double discrimination because of race and sexual preference. They are probably the most isolated group of people in America. Black homosexuals are rejected by blacks because of sexual preference and by the white society on the grounds of race and sexual preference. Christian counselors need to be empathic toward this double assault on their counselees' self-esteem. For the individual who is black, a latent homosexual, and a Christian, the guilt, confusion, and inner conflicts are an enormous burden to bear. The function of Christian counselors regarding gay people is to furnish a supportive therapeutic environment that neither condemns nor condones their behavior. Christian latent homosexuals may enter counseling with other issues until they feel comfortable enough to risk disclosing the issue of sexuality. Sometimes symptoms mask the problem as in the following case example.

> Darwin was a twenty-nine-year-old black man who quit his job as a lab technician working with human semen at a prestigious university. After a while he began to develop an irrational dread that he would catch AIDS. Darwin came to

therapy with his phobia regarding AIDS as the presenting problem. He began compulsively washing his hands several times per day. He bathed himself with Lysol disinfectant and often insisted that his girlfriend do the same. He also ritualistically wiped door knobs he thought had been contaminated.

Darwin's history revealed that he grew up overprotected and smothered by his mother and his sister, who had a great deal of influence upon him. The counselor also discovered that Darwin had a sexual experience with a cousin at the age of eight in which they wrestled in the nude and rubbed each other's genitalia.

Darwin experienced a tremendous amount of anxiety with respect to AIDS and guilt about his own sexuality. After several sessions of tracking his behavior and reviewing information obtained in counseling, it became clear that Darwin was more concerned about gay men than about AIDS. He frequently talked about dread of shaking hands with gay men and of being in close proximity to them. It became apparent that he was a young black Christian undergoing intrapersonal conflicts regarding his own latent homosexuality. He clung to his girlfriend, became involved in a few premarital sexual episodes with her, and felt tremendous guilt afterward. She provided him with a sense of his own masculinity. When she threatened to break off the relationship, he would hound her until she took him back.

Much of Darwin's anxiety was in the realm of the unconscious. The therapeutic approach with him was not to push him to examine his sexual conflict at first, but to work with him on his phobic reaction to AIDS. A relationship was constructed of brotherly Christian love where he would feel comfortable enough to share. Also, work building his self-esteem slowly began to show him how his behavior revealed his latent fears. Darwin began to discover his real fear was not so much AIDS but fear that he himself was gay. At first he resisted the interpretation and proceeded to try to justify his AIDS phobia. His anxiety level was very high. Because of his obsessive-compulsive nature it was clear that further exploration should be postponed until he was ready. At the end of the sessions, Darwin saw that gay men had been the real issue for him even more than AIDS.

This kind of incident may occur when dealing with a Christian who is struggling with unresolved feelings regarding homosexuality.

Gary Collins suggests that counselors determine realistic goals in relation to what the counselee wants; instill a realistic hope; share knowledge to dispel any myths counselees may have about their homosexuality; show love and acceptance of the person; encourage behavior change; and recognize that counseling may be complex.[3]

To these suggestions, I would add that counselors give attention to black homosexuals' experiences of discrimination rooted in ethnicity and sexual preference. They may suffer low self-esteem, resulting in suicidal depression. In addition, practitioners should seek an audience with the homosexuals' families to discuss family issues concerning the counselees' homosexuality. However, a family consultation should not occur unless both counselees and their families are ready for such an assembly, and there exists genuine family concerns around the issue of homosexuality. Christian counselors must also be careful not to assume that because persons have admitted to same-sex encounters they are homosexuals. In the African-American community, where men and women are acculturated to sex earlier in general than whites, it is not uncommon for men and women to have engaged in a same-sex experience while exploring their sexuality as youngsters. The best advice is to refrain from hasty assumptions until sufficient information has been obtained.

From time to time counselors may be confronted with those who bring other forms of sexual behavior to counseling, such as incest, transvestism, sexual fetishes, sexual masochism, sexual sadism, or pedophilia. When such issues exceed the scope of the counselor's professional ability, do not hesitate to refer the counselee to an appropriate mental health professional.

One other sexual condition that prompts a small number of blacks to seek treatment is hypersexuality. Here again caution is the rule since hypersexuality, like beauty, is in the eye of the beholder. A wife complaining that her husband has an excessive sexual appetite may in fact be cloaking her own inhibited desire. On the other hand, there may be those whose sexual activity may indeed be categorized as hypersexual. This condition includes

1. Manic episodes (sudden changes in behavior)
2. Drug-induced psychotic states
3. Borderline personality (those who use excessive behavior in a particular way to fill emptiness and to give themselves a feeling of personal identity)
4. Reaction formation to orgasmic inhibitions[4]

Hypersexuality requires psychiatric intervention and here again Christian counselors should not hesitate to refer clients to psychiatrists. Although hypersexuality is a condition that can appear in any ethnic group, it is stereotypically attributed to the sexuality of black people due to certain myths concerning them Such myths often interfere with relationships between husbands and wives as well as counselors and counselees. Therefore, these myths must be exposed and dispelled by the therapist.

SEXUAL MYTHS AND STEREOTYPES

Unfortunately, among other things, blacks have been the victims of stereotypes with respect to their sexuality. Men have been cast for the role of "studs" who possess suprahuman sexual powers. Black women are portrayed as oversexed "harlots" waiting to release their unrestrained sensuality at the slightest urging. False stories regarding the size of the black male's sexual organ have endured from the time of slavery to the present. White males feel threatened by these legends and have historically taken serious measures (lynching, castration, and discriminatory legislation) to protect white women.

Even black men have succumbed to myths about their sexual abilities. For many black men these myths engender a sense of pride. In their view, they could finally do something the white man could not. Staples writes, "Since Black men were unable to achieve status in the work place they have exercised the privilege of their manliness and attempted to achieve it in the bedroom."[5]

The truth is, these perceptions are erroneous. Black men do not possess any special sexual abilities, and black women are not oversexed harlots. There is no significant difference in the genitalia of black and white men. White and black men are very much alike in that their sexuality varies from person to person. Young black men, however, do seem to be more sexually active than young white men. But this is because young black men hold more liberal attitudes toward sex and are socialized earlier—all as a result of cultural conditioning and not innate sexuality.

Christian practitioners, both black and white, must examine their own beliefs and attitudes in relation to the sexuality of black people. They must determine what, if any, stereotypical myths are part of their own intellectual motif. If counselors believe the same myths as counselees, their ability to help them is significantly reduced. Once this issue is settled, counselors will be in a position to assist in dispelling the falsities about sexuality. Christian counselors must enable black counselees to identify the sexual myths they have been operating on, provide them with more accurate information, help black males explore other means by which their masculinity can be expressed, and instruct them toward a healthful, Christian view of sex.

THE CHRISTIAN VIEW OF SEX

Of all the people in the world, Christians should possess the most accurate understanding of sex because of our relationship with the God who created us. But this is not always the case. Believers may be as sexually traumatized as anyone else. If they came from homes where sex was not openly discussed, or grew up in an environment where Victorian ideals were the norm, the result is often a repressive view of sex. Christians must adhere to a proper biblical perspective on sex, especially if they intend to counsel others.

What is an appropriate, biblical understanding of sex? Herbert Miles argues that it should include five principles based on 1 Thessalonians 4:1–8:

> God instituted marriage and the sexual nature of marriage; each man is to select his own wife (each woman her own

husband); the motive for selection must be characterized by personal purity and concern for total life relationship; to allow sexual passions alone to guide one in selecting a mate, as pagans do, is unclean and a violation of the will of God; and by entering marriage the right way one performs the will of God.[6]

Moreover, Miles states that God created sex to be a personally pleasurable relationship for both husband and wife.[7] I would add that, for married couples, sex should be governed by four biblical postulates. First, the relationship should be informed by sexual knowledge. In Genesis 4:1 we read "Adam knew his wife." Although the Scriptures are referring to the sexual act, in a very real sense Adam knew Eve in an intimate way. He knew her spiritually as well as sexually, which is what many black men who come to counseling do not know. They are often ignorant concerning the physical, emotional, and spiritual nature of female sexuality. If black men are functioning out of sexual myths, they may not recognize the need for such knowledge and black women may demur from challenging them on the issue. Nevertheless, in a biblical sense, knowledge is power when it comes to sex.

Second, sex in marriage should have sexual novelty. The Bible tells us that "marriage is honourable . . . and the bed undefiled" (Hebrews 13:4). Since God's Word is true, whatever married couples do upon their beds that is mutually gratifying is permissible. This is where our Victorian values may harm us. Such values cause couples to be one-dimensional. Some Christians have a rather prosaic sex life that is not consistent with Scripture (Proverbs 5:19; Song of Solomon 7:6–9; 1 Corinthians 7:3–5). Couples need to experiment more and be adventuresome in sexual expression with each other.

Third, sexual relations should be frequent. This is clear from the following passages: "Let her breasts satisfy thee at all times; and be thou ravished always with her love" (Proverb 5:19); and "Defraud ye not one the other, except it be with consent for a time, that ye may give yourselves to fasting and prayer; and come together again, that Satan tempt you not for your incontinency" (1 Corinthians 7:5). We see from these verses that the consistency of sexual relations is encouraged.

Finally, sexual fidelity is a principle that must govern the marital bond. African-American believers should be appalled by the position of many professional blacks who are advocating mate sharing as an acceptable alternative for black single women, given the low supply of eligible single black men. This notion is immoral and impractical. The solution to the black male shortage is not mate sharing but Christ sharing. Black Christians must make a concerted effort to win black men in the jails and on street corners to Christ. And until the tide of black male homicide, the leading killer of our young men between the ages of fifteen and thirty, is reversed we will still have a shortage of single men. The idea of mate sharing typifies the extent to which secular humanism has infiltrated the ranks of professional blacks. God forbid that such a practice should become accepted by the black community. It is nothing less than sanctioned adultery and fornication. God's Word is clear about these trespasses in the context of marriage. We see this in passages such as 1 Corinthians 7:2—"let every man have his own wife, and let every woman have her own husband." Ironically, it is the violation of sexual fidelity that ultimately motivates black couples to seek counseling. Since no other issue forces African-Americans into therapy more often, greater attention needs to be given to the issue of extramarital affairs.

Issues surrounding sexuality are important for another reason. They lead to power and control struggles in marital interaction. Of this matter Goldberg states:

> Because of the circular nature of couple interaction both members of the couple will sooner or later feed into the causative processes. Couples in which the man, for instance, will want to have sex daily and the woman in reaction will not only decline the daily schedule, but will resort to a position of withholding sex almost entirely. In such couples the sexual interaction becomes a forum for power and control struggles.[8]

NOTES

[1]Staples, *Black Masculinity*, 7–8.

[2]Lynn Norment, "The Truth About AIDS," *Ebony* (April 1987): 126.

[3]Collins, *Christian Counseling*, 324.

[4]Martin Goldberg, "Understanding Hypersexuality in Men and Women," *Intergrating Sex and Marital Therapy: A Clinical Guide*, eds. Gerald R. Weeks and Larry Hot (New York: Bronner/Mazel, 1987), 202–19.

[5]Staples, *Black Masculinity*, 85.

[6]Herbert J. Miles, *Sexual Happinesss in Marriage: A Christian Interpretation of Sexual Adjustment in Marriage* (Grand Rapids: Zondervan, 1972), 33–49.

[7]Ibid.

[8]Goldberg, "Understanding Hypersexuality," 202–19.

4

POWER ISSUES

"Of great authority" (Acts 8:27)

A fourth issue faced by Philip as he sought to relate to the black man from Ethiopia was the issue of power. Acts 8:27 shows that the Ethiopian was a eunuch of great authority under Candace, queen of Ethiopia. He was a man in a position of power higher than most of the men of his nation. But that authority was subject to a black woman who held even more power. We may surmise that this did not threaten the ego of the eunuch and that he was comfortable reporting to Candace.

The same cannot be said for scores of black men in the United States who have been a rather powerless group. They may view any subservience to today's black Candaces as an affront to their masculine integrity. Yet a challenge to black masculinity is precisely the situation that the feminist movement has brought to black men.

POWERLESSNESS AND THE BLACK MALE

The feminist movement has brought profound changes in the ways that men and women relate to each other. Sociologist John Scanzoni notes:

> The feminist movement succeeded in creating a class-consciousness in women which the by-products of their struggles and conflicts gradually filtered, ad hoc fashion, into the institution of marriage which caused structural changes that have led to worldwide increases in divorce. The changes

have increased favorably for wives and less favorably for husbands in terms of rights, privileges, duties, and obligations.[1]

George Gilder, in his book *Sexual Suicide*, further argues that "the feminist movement is the greatest enemy to black progress in America. It influentially opposes programs that are crucial to reestablishing the black male as chief providers and supporter of his family."[2]

An employer can satisfy gender and ethnic requirements in hiring a black woman. Should a hiring choice be between a male or a female, employers often hire the black woman. The loser once again is the black man. The scene is now set for the struggle for power and control between husbands and wives. Black men quantify power in terms of economics. They are threatened by the potential loss of more power from none other than their own women.

This negative feature of feminism is even more apparent from the research of Bernadette Gray-Little, who gathered data from seventy-five married couples from urban North Carolina. The couples were drawn from several predominantly black sections of the city and were chosen on the basis of census tract and black statistics to represent a wide variety of backgrounds. The study investigated the effects of spousal-power distribution affecting marital quality among black couples. It was demonstrated that husband-led power patterns were associated in general with the highest levels of marital quality. The results showed that greatest satisfaction was found among couples in traditional relationships. The research suggests blacks in this sampling prefer more traditional husband-led homes.[3]

My practice involves hundreds of hours as a marriage counselor, with a case load of ninety percent black Christian couples, supports the finding of Gray-Little. Born-again black couples tend to prefer the husband-led home taught in Ephesians 5. While this evidence is not conclusive, it does show that a segment of the black population finds satisfaction in marriages that establish traditional homes according to Judaeo-Christian values.

It is for these couples that the impact of feminist thinking may prove most disruptive since, generally speaking, black couples maintain a more egalitarian relationship in marriage than do whites. This marital parity is partly a function of the socio-economic status and education level of the black male. There is a correlation between black male power in the home and socio-economics. Scanzoni found that as the black male brings more economic status to the family, the more he perceives his own authority to increase. From the wife's viewpoint, her authority is increased when her husband has only limited education. If education is considered a resource that the black husband uses to bargain for authority in the family, the less of it he has the more authority the wife perceives she ought to possess. Where couples have similar levels of education the tension may be keen as each spouse pushes to tip the authority scale to his or her favor. In such couples constant arguing, bickering, and power jockeying are a common occurrence. The following case illustrates a black Christian couple's power and control struggle that emerged as one of their patterns.

> Raymond was thirty-one years old and employed as a traveling representative for the phone company. Charon, his wife, was thirty-two and employed as a social worker. Raymond had a bachelor's degree and Charon had her master's degree. They had been married about two years and had a little boy about seven months old.

> The presenting problem was that the couple had been experiencing a considerable amount of conflict around Charon's decision to have her own savings account separate from Raymond. Presently, the couple had all accounts jointly in both their names. However, Raymond's propensity for writing checks that bounced and not keeping good records had gotten the couple into some financial trouble. Charon decided she was going to take control of her life by opening her own account to which Raymond would not have access. This did not sit well with Raymond, who saw Charon's move as an attempt to undermine his authority. He stated that if she was going to insist on having this separate account, then maybe the account ought not to be the only thing to separate. It was his opinion that no money should be kept from him and that all funds should be under his purview as

the husband. Charon felt that all money keeping should be turned over to her because she was a better manager.

The two were fairly cordial to each other in the session, but it was clear they were pretty entrenched in their respective positions and consequently reached an impasse. Fortunately, the couple did not have a lot of grievous problems other than power and control issues. They were able to talk to each other and were good candidates for communication-skills training. This training was combined with family-of-origin work. Charon realized that she was following a power script from her family of origin where women were all independently strong and functioned as main power brokers in her family. Raymond, on the other hand, came from a family in which his mother held the power. After a few sessions Raymond was able to see how he had deep resentment toward his mother's dominance over his father. He realized some of his conflict with Charon stemmed from his fear of losing power and being dominated the way his father was. Ironically, Raymond married a woman who was just like his mother. This couple was now able to see that their own power issues came from their family-of-origin scripts.

So far we have discussed power issues of the black male. But the black female is, in some ways, more powerless than the male. Her unique experience of powerlessness deserves attention.

POWERLESSNESS AND THE BLACK FEMALE

Powerlessness in the black female may take a number of forms. Powerlessness may show itself in a marital situation in which the woman's needs have been all but neglected in favor of those of her husband. She becomes little more than a live-in domestic and concubine for her dishonoring mate. She rarely, if at all, has any input into the major decisions of the home, and is generally relegated to the role of tacit supporter. This woman often adheres to the scriptural tenet "wives, submit yourselves unto your own husbands" (Ephesians 5:22). And in some cases, she uses this verse to justify enduring physical abuse at the hands of her husband. Usually she cannot leave because of her economic dependency on the man, the desire to keep the family together, or her own religious beliefs regarding separation and divorce. When she does not perform some task to the liking of her mate, she is promptly put back in her place by the husband's threats of leaving, withholding of economic privileges, moral tongue lashings, or physical assault.

Add to all of this the superwoman syndrome many black women exhibit trying to balance the roles of mother, wife, and employee. And their sense of powerlessness is very real. One might think that being in the workplace is a way for black women to increase their power. But they may become victims of double discrimination on the job, being both black and female. Proportionately, they are the lowest paid racial, sexual group.

Many women turn their incomes over to husbands, who in turn may give them some kind of meager living allowance.

If a black woman is a single parent, she is usually a member of the poorest family in America. With no man to support her and few financial resources, she often turns to the only recourse available to her—public assistance.[4]

Another way in which black women feel powerless is when they possess power traditionally ascribed to men, but are conflicted about exercising it. An example of this is the married black woman whose family of origin gives women the authority in the home even though men were present. She has learned to be the dominant person in power. This type of woman usually gravitates toward men who have passive-dependent needs and gladly give up power.

This sort of match may work well for many couples. However, if the wife is a born-again Christian and has been exposed to teaching on God's order for the family, she may find herself in somewhat of a bind. On the one hand, she knows her husband should be the head and make the final decisions. On the other hand, she knows she is the real power in the home. This woman is not anxious to relinquish power that brings her certain rewards. Thus, she has power that gratifies her female ego while at the same time causes a lot of guilt. At times she may find herself stuck—wanting badly to take charge of a situation yet fighting desperately to restrain herself so that her husband can take the lead. The situation may be even more complicated by the woman feeling that her husband is neither capable nor competent to make certain decisions. This is a form of powerlessness that is power without clear sanctions—it is ambivalent power. Such powerlessness is not confined to the home, but may extend to the job where black women are in positions of authority over men. There are messages she may receive both directly or indirectly concerning the limitations of her power.

Christian counselors need to be aware of the power issues for black men and women and intervene appropriately when these dynamics exhibit themselves in therapy.

CHRISTIAN COUNSELING AND POWERLESSNESS

Given the previous discussion, one question that all of this raises concerns what Christian counselors can do in the face of powerlessness. Christian counselors need to help black counselees deal with their sense of powerlessness by pointing out the negative effects it has on their relationships as couples and their lives as individuals. Christian counselors can help couples to rethink what power is and how it is to be used. For instance, to the husband of the woman who feels powerless because of the misunderstood passage, "wives, submit yourselves unto your own husbands," counselors may be able to assist him to see that her submission is to a loving husband in the context of the love of Christ. Such men do not suppress the rights of their wives, but give themselves up as Christ did for the church so that those rights might be protected. Counselors can point out to black males that power needs to be shared. Using our Lord as an example, counselors can show black men that though Christ has all power he shares that power with his bride, the church, and makes her his joint heir (Romans 8:17).

With a dominating black wife, counselors can reframe her power in such a way that she can use it to assist her husband to become the head of the household. Such a woman may need to make a distinction between power (the ability to influence the actions of others) and position. Counselors can enable her to understand that she does not have to relinquish such power, but can use it to bolster her husband's position. The aim is help her to utilize her influence for God's purposes. This approach is less threatening to a black woman more accustomed to role reversal where women head the home. If she can comprehend that she has been able to influence a dependent spouse to be less dependent and more in line with God's order for the home, that woman has utilized real power in accordance with her role as God's helpmeet to her husband.

The role of socio-economics is a basis for power and control struggles in marital interaction. Socio-economic issues are probably the second leading cause of marital conflict among black couples. It is another issue that deserves special focus.

NOTES

[1]John Scanzoni, *Sexual Bargaining: Power Politics in the American Marriage* (Englewood Cliffs: Prentice Hall, 1972), 31–37.

[2]George F. Gilder, *Sexual Suicide* (New York: Bantam, 1975), 129.

[3]Bernadette Gray-Little, "Marital Quality and Power Processes Among Black Couples," *Journal of Marriage and the Family* (August 1982): 129.

[4]*Ebony* (August 1986).

5

SOCIO-ECONOMIC ISSUES

"Who had the charge of all her treasure" (Acts 8:27)

As we continue to review Acts 8:27, we see another fact about the eunuch—he had "the charge of all her treasure." The man from Ethiopia was responsible for the queen's money. Philip was dealing with a man of high political position who wielded a great deal of socioeconomic influence in his country. The economic status of the eunuch was another issue Philip encountered as he sought to relate to this man.

Christian counselors face this issue when they deal with black counselees. It affects the familial structure of the black family and, as we have already discussed, the power struggles between black men and women. The ways in which African-Americans respond to socioeconomic pressure are useful knowledge for Christian counselors.

SOCIO-ECONOMICS AND BLACK FAMILY STRUCTURE

We have seen in the first chapter that the black family demonstrates amazing adaptive flexibility. This flexibility of the familial structure is in response to economics. The multigenerational structure of black families is often a response to economic pressures. Thus, two and three generations will often live in the same house, pool their resources and share bills. It is not uncommon for in-laws, parents, siblings, and grandparents to come to the aid of a family member experiencing financial difficulties.

A single-parent black woman may deliberately not marry her paramour because she may acquire more support from welfare than she would if he had a job. Many single blacks may stay with parents or other relatives for financial reasons, perhaps especially the high costs of rent.

Whatever the financial pressures on the black counselee, there is usually some kind of adaptive response. That response may be a two-edged sword—it may reduce economic pressure while increasing interfamilial conflicts. Counselors need to assess the kinds of adaptation black counselees have made and identify the hardships these engender. Men especially may experience considerable personal anguish about unemployment. Unable to provide for their families, they may even leave their families so that their wives will be able to obtain support from public assistance. If a counselor does not understand that family structuring for African-Americans is often an adaptation to economic conditions, these husbands will be viewed as men who abandoned their responsibilities because they did not care. George Gilder stated the importance of employment to black men: The chief requirement for giving upward mobility to any poor community is maintenance of a family and employment structure that affirms the male in his provider role.[1]

On the other hand, there is the employment of black women. Out of necessity they are forced into the workplace to help support their families because their husband's pay checks are inadequate for the needs of the family. But they discover that there is no child-care support if a relative is unavailable. This results in many women giving up their jobs at a time when two incomes are a necessity. Robert Taylor contends that middle-class blacks often show the same multigenerational patterns as lower-class blacks.[2]

SOCIO-ECONOMICS AND MARITAL SATISFACTION

For black couples, there is a relationship between marital satisfaction and economics. The more satisfied wives are with their economic situation, the more satisfied they are with their marriage. The more contented black husbands are with job rewards, the more likely they are to maintain their marriage.[3]

Marital satisfaction is contingent upon the degree to which each spouse's economic expectations are fulfilled. These expectations differ along gender lines.

Black men have three economic concerns. First, having a job helps them feel they are responsible men earning a decent living.

Second, black men are concerned about being accepted on their jobs without discrimination, commended for doing good work, and feeling as though they are making a significant contribution. In addition, they want salaries and benefits commensurate with the work they are doing. Unfortunately, racism in the workplace prevents this from happening in many cases.

Finally, black men are concerned about how money is spent, and they need certain restraints on spending. Black women, however, also have three economic concerns. The first is basic sustenance. Since many of them grew up in impoverished homes, they resort to marriage to escape poverty. Therefore, at minimum, they feel deserving of food, clothing, and shelter and do not want to be in a position where fundamental needs are a daily worry.

Second, black women, like white women, are esthetically perceptive. They enjoy looking at attractive objects. This is more a gender issue than racial, for it was the woman in Genesis who saw that the tree was "pleasant to the eyes" (Genesis 3:6). Women like to look at pretty things, and it is natural for them to desire such commodities. But black men, who are struggling to provide sufficient income to meet necessities, may not be so enthusiastic to buy these extra items they deem luxuries.

Finally, black women are concerned about future inheritance, that is, what happens to them and their children in the event of the husband's death. Many women come from families or know of others where a black man died leaving his family with few resources to sustain them.

Because economic concerns vary between black men and women, it is easy to see how money disputes can create tension in relationships, as illustrated by the following case.

Deidra and Burt are a young Christian couple who came to therapy because Burt threatened to leave the relationship over constant arguing about money. He was very reluctant to come to therapy, and it was difficult to engage him in the initial part of the session. Burt was twenty-six and unemployed as an insurance agent. Deidra was twenty-six and an unemployed student finishing up law school. The couple was staying with Deidra's mother until they could get on their feet. This presented problems between Burt and his mother-in-law. She would put pressure on Deidra, who put pressure on Burt, about paying more rent and taking on some of the other bills of the home. Burt was very resentful about this and wanted to get out of the home as soon as possible. In addition, he had a problem with Deidra's spending habits. In his mind, she did not seem to understand why they could not buy certain things even though they were living only off his salary of about $15,000 per year.

Deidra on the other hand felt that Burt was insensitive, stingy, and uncaring for her needs. She believed it was his responsibility to care for her.

This couple did not have good communication skills. Deidra was an expressive talker who did not give Burt much of an opportunity to share. Burt rarely established eye contact and discounted whatever Deidra said.

The first task was to try to change this pattern to get them to listen to each other. This involved getting Deidra to talk less and Burt to talk more.

Second, we identified economic concerns as one of the issues to discuss. We discussed how the pressures they faced as young black Christians were real and common, but that they needed to try to understand each other's different concerns regarding finances. I pointed out to Deidra that some of her financial expectations needed to be postponed. I also explained to Burt that Deidra had some concerns he needed to appreciate. And I mentioned to them that, from a biblical perspective, they must learn to be more swift to hear and slow to speak and, in the spirit of Ephesians, they should learn to submit themselves one to another (Ephesians 5:21).

It took an entire session but they both agreed to work on these issues. I suggested they discuss a plan for moving into their own place to ease the tensions with Deidra's mother.

The aim here was to help the couple, especially Deidra, become freer of her mother. I had to be cautious because I did not want Deidra to cut off her mother who had been a big help in supporting the couple.

I suggested that while they were still living there some equitable compromise be worked out with Deidra's mother about their financial responsibility. This helped Burt to understand that his mother-in-law, as a divorced woman, did have some legitimate concerns about having to carry the financial weight. They were encouraged to work together and pool resources as a family and follow biblical plans concerning use of their money. I asked Deidra to consider a part-time job to help take some of the pressure off the situation until they got on their feet. The couple accepted the plan and agreed to work on this in the next sessions.

This is an example of some of the financial issues black couples may have concerning economics and how they respond to financial pressures.

Socio-economics is responsible for the determination of another important issue—environment. Scientists tell us that what a person becomes is connected to the interplay of heredity and environment. It is prudent for counselors to find out what impact environment has on the African-Americans they serve in counseling.

NOTES

[1]Gilder, *Sexual Suicide*, 129.
[2]Taylor, *Receipt of Support*.
[3]Scanzoni, *Black Families in Modern Society*, 226.

6

ENVIRONMENTAL ISSUES

"And had come to Jerusalem" (Acts 8:27)

Returning to Acts 8:27, we see that the eunuch had come to Jerusalem. He had moved from one kind of social environment to another, a place with one kind of metropolitan subculture to a place with a different kind of subculture.

Where black counselees have moved from one environment to a different one, whether an urban setting to a suburban or rural setting, for example, such a move in some way impinges on them in therapy. It is imperative to assess this aspect of a counselee's life. There are two kinds of environment dimensions that require attention: the home environment and the community environment.

HOME ENVIRONMENTAL INFLUENCES

The first environment to which we are exposed after birth is the home. It is one that conveys powerful messages to us. When environment is an issue in counseling, the counselor must ask questions such as these: How many people are in the house relative to space? How much privacy does each member have? Do persons have their own bedrooms or do they share? Is the home a single family dwelling or multifamily dwelling? Is the decor colorful or drab? Is the lighting bright or dull? What is the usual temperature? Is the home clean and orderly? Are vermin or pests in the home? Are pets? What kind of traffic patterns exist? What kind of conveniences exist? Is the home open or closed? Does the artwork in the home suggest that it is Christian or non-Christian? What are the most common odors and fragrances?

Home environment is more than a physical structure with dimensions; it also has psychosocial impact. For example, one needs to ascertain, whether the home was rowdy or tranquil? Was the emotional milieu highly charged with feelings or was it more low key? What were the family rituals? Was there a pattern of family devotions in the home? Many blacks come from homes where several people lived in the same household. Space and privacy were unattainable luxuries, given the nature of family interaction. Vermin and pests were present on a daily basis. The home was often in need of major repairs that the family could not afford. Furthermore, the home was often a forum for angry emotions and feelings. For many, it was a place where the smell of alcohol, tobacco, or marijuana was a common occurrence.

Yet there are other homes that, while not affluent in appearance, are immaculate. The family eats together, prays together, and aromas of fine ethnic cuisine fill the house. It is obvious that if two people from these very different home backgrounds come together in marriage, sooner or later the issue of environment is bound to emerge in counseling. Further, some individuals may have made several moves, with all of the different environmental issues that each move brings. The following case is an example:

> Sharon is a thirty-one-year-old black divorcée and single parent. She is a born again believer who has been a Christian for about four years. She has two children—a boy aged seven and a girl aged five. The son lives with his grandparents in Virginia and the daughter with Sharon.

> Sharon came into therapy because she was feeling depressed about her life. She had been treated in therapy when she was sixteen. She had a very enmeshed relationship with her mother and had been judged by the family as the depressed, crazy one. She was married for seven years, and divorced her husband because of abuse and extramarital affairs. The divorce put her in financial straits. So Sharon moved from an urban setting to a more rural setting to live with her parents.

Staying with her parents brought an abrupt environmental change. First of all, it meant giving up her own home to move into her parents' home. This produced conflict with her mother who tried to dominate Sharon's life. Sharon moved out of her parents' house after a brief stay, and her own apartment after finding a job. Her parents decided to help her by keeping her children while she worked.

Sharon met a man on the job with whom she became involved and with whom she lived in his apartment. The relationship went sour after two years. Sharon returned with her daughter to the city to live with a sister. Until Sharon could find a job and bring her son to live with her and his sister, the boy remained with her parents, where he attended school.

The environment of her sister's home was one in which Sharon had little space. There was only one bed in the room where she slept, so she and her daughter slept in the same bed. In addition, her sister's teenage son constantly harassed Sharon and her daughter with verbal abuse and intimidation. Although this had been brought to the attention of her sister and her sister's husband, the harassment continued. The sister and husband were in the process of a divorce and constantly argued and yelled. Their arguing was easily heard through the thin walls. Sharon bought her own food, put it in the one refrigerator in the home, and often found it eaten by her nephew. This environmental situation kept her depressed and angry.

There are a lot of issues in this case with respect to the counselee's family relationships and her own intrapsychic dynamics. However, it is also clear that her situation is complicated by the number of major moves she has made in addition to the environmental influences of her sister's residence.

Home environment plays an important role in terms of family pressures, values, and expectations. Home environment (what happens inside the door) and community environment (what happens outside the door) are formidable forces in shaping human behavior. There are any number of ways counselees can respond to such forces as each finds his own novel adaptability.

COMMUNITY ENVIRONMENTAL INFLUENCES

It is vital that information about the nature of the community environment counselees grew up in and of their present residence be secured by Christian counselors. If counselees have been living in a rural southern town (as many blacks have) and have traveled to a large urban city, they may experience displacement, alienation, and cultural shock.

Each neighborhood within black communities has its own sense of identity, their own kind of subculture, and their own perception of who is "in" and who is "out" of that community. The language of a neighborhood is communicated by the physical aspects of the neighborhood—by the structure of the housing, as rowhouses, twin apartments, condos, or single homes; the landscape—trees and grass, or old tires converted into flower pots; and by the neighborhood events whether young ebony girls jumping double-dutch in trash-strewn streets or boys playing baseball on a well-manicured ball field. Each community sends potent signals to its constituents. In the black community it is common for those signals to be negative. If the area is a high-crime area, a red-light district, a haven for pimps and addicts, or prey for burglars, robbers and felons, a person growing up in such an area is exposed to that neighborhood's message and makes the necessary behavioral adjustments to cope.

Christian counselors have a responsibility beyond mere assessment of the impact of the home and community environment. Through the use of Scripture they must enable black counselees to change environmental elements that are changeable, and to accept those that are not subject to change.

To alter any milieu requires energy. And energy requires hope. Very often African-Americans come into counseling hopeless, feeling futile concerning their ability to make things different. This is one of the first things that needs to be addressed. Our counselees must be reminded that the origin of true hope is not to be found outside of oneself. For "hope that is seen is not hope" (Romans 8:24). How true this is for many African-Americans when they look for hope beyond themselves in their home and community environments. On the basis of what they see, they conclude that there is not much hope. The hope that they seek is deferred, and "hope deferred maketh the heart sick" (Proverbs 13:12). A sick heart is what we counselors refer to as neurosis, psychosis, pathology, or emotional disorder. All are to one degree or another manifestations of the sick heart. Minority counselees often fall prey to a vicious cycle of intrapersonal and interpersonal problems stemming from such sick hearts. The sick heart develops when hope for a major change has not happened. Hope is deferred because the counselee is looking for a hope that is visible. Christian counselors must help black counselees break this cycle of hopelessness by enabling them to see that hope must come from within one who has accepted Christ as Savior and Lord. Counselees must come to the realization that it is Christ in them who is "the hope of glory" (Colossians 1:27). People who understand this revelation are ready to invest energy in changing the things in their environment that can be changed, for the glory of God, for the betterment of themselves, their families and their communities.

I do not agree with those who think resolutions to the problems of African-Americans lie solely in changing the social forces that shape our environment. Changes in society must begin with an individual—start at the micro-level and radiate out to the macro-level. Therefore, a black man who has received the power of Christ can in turn change his home and community by that same power. It was this power that prompted the people of the New Testament era to say of the apostles that these are they "that have turned the world upside down" (Acts 17:6). That power is available to blacks. With a new found hope in Christ they can take on negative environments and turn them upside down for God.

It is for this reason that Christian counselors must get in touch with the religious lives of black counselees. For it is there that the greatest potential and vitality for change exist.

7

RELIGIOUS ISSUES

"Had come to Jerusalem for to worship" (Acts 8:27)

Philip discovered the Ethiopian eunuch had gone to Jerusalem to worship (Acts 8:27). We learn that the Ethiopian was a pious man, and had an awareness of God. And while he did not possess complete understanding, he at least knew enough about this Deity to want to worship and learn about him by reading Isaiah. Of all the facts surrounding Philip's encounter with the eunuch, this one provided him with the entree into the Ethiopian's chariot. Just as religion played a significant role in the life of a black man in the story of Acts 8, it is also an important feature in the history of African-Americans today.

THE CHRISTIAN FAITH AS A STRENGTH OF BLACK FAMILIES

To discuss black religion one must discuss the black church, the most vibrant institution in the black community. As such, it is the institution most responsible for the survival of black people in this country. Concerning the role of the black church and its relationship to survival of African-Americans, Robert Staples says that it has been a "buffer institution which provided many blacks with an outlet for their frustrations in a society which penalized them daily for their racial membership."[1]

Cobbs and Grier, in their book *The Jesus Bag*, note that the misery of African-American life was too much to endure, so they reached into religious experience to extract a black mystique—a soul. They used the weapon of religion to survive an attack on their lives. African-Americans took a Jesus bag shaped like a noose and reshaped it into a black cornucopia of spiritual riches.[2] Their capacity for converting weakness into strength was nowhere more evident than in religion.

While the black church must be lauded for its indispensable contributions to the survival of African-Americans, it has not been without its shortcomings. Christian counselors cannot assume that just because black people have a religious background they have received sound biblical teaching. In reality the opposite may be true. Counselees may be biblical illiterates without a good working knowledge of Scripture. The Ethiopian eunuch stands as a classic symbol for the spiritual condition of many black Christians who read Isaiah but do not understand what they are reading. This situation is the product of the kind of teaching and preaching often characteristic of the black church. Harriet Pipes McAdoo says a typical black church service "is not an intellectual occasion and not a time for thinking. The problem becomes one of arousing the emotions, and of helping the tired, subleveled black person to associate his or her trials of sorrows and joys with those of biblical characters."[3]

If black preachers are not arousing the emotions through passionate sermons, they may evoke an emotional response through the social gospel approach. Of this type of preaching William Banks states: "The black social gospel preacher is fond of spotting the sins of the white power structure, and there is much talk about the sins of society and corporate guilt. However, little is said about the sins of the individuals who make up their congregations."[4] Banks suggests that this "failure to preach the gospel has helped produce a people who cannot discern right from wrong. Even though they are church members, they are Bible illiterates unable to discern God's will for their personal lives."[5]

The essence of this discussion is that there are spiritual deficits counselees bring to the session to which Christian counselors may need to attend.

SPIRITUAL AND BIBLICAL NEEDS OF BLACKS

There are certain spiritual needs that blacks bring to counseling. As mentioned above, many black counselees may not have a good understanding of Scripture concerning the plan of salvation and God's forgiveness. They may be experiencing deep guilt for past sins they concluded were outside of God's scope of forgiveness. They may also exhibit defensive mechanisms to cover up painful guilt that proceeds from an erroneous image of God as an unloving, punitive father. This may be particularly true for those influenced by holiness churches. Bruce Narramore suggests Christian counselors need to help the counselee

> loosen unnecessarily rigid, stringent, neurotic or God-like goals, and to focus on the conflicts and sinfulness hidden beneath the defense patterns. This approach encourages a mature self-evaluative process that leads to facing the origins of neurotic guilt, and increases a sense of authenticity and a healthy remorse or godly sorrow.[6]

Counselors must help black counselees differentiate false guilt from real guilt. When there is real guilt, Quentin Hyder says,

> breaking God's law can only be dealt with by eternal separation from him or by repentance leading to forgiveness and reconciliation. This and only this can totally remove the burden of guilt from the sinner. No psychotherapy of any sort can effectively remove true guilt. Only forgiveness by the man who has been wronged or God who has been sinned against can do this. True guilt is both a legal and theological issue.[7]

Second, blacks often suffer from a complex similar to the experiences of the biblical character of Job. They adhere to a suffering theology in which they see God involved in all the misfortunes that befall them. While such a theology may have merit in terms of enabling one to handle calamity, if not balanced by the concept of a caring heavenly Father, it can also lead to false conclusions about God. Counselors can help them obtain a balanced view that they might have life and have it more abundantly.

Third, other theological ideas that emanate from faulty Bible teaching may require challenging, such as the notion of salvation based on works; the belief that blacks are victims of the Hamitic curse (Genesis 9:25); a reliance on anathema in the form of dreams; signs and individual revelations; and a penchant for enobling ministers to the point of personality cultism. Christian counselors must not be apprehensive about exploring these beliefs with blacks. They should feel comfortable and competent in discussing spiritual things. Too often there is a failure to do this, as James Griffith noted:

> Therapists are uncomfortable opening therapy to the religious realm and thus exclude religion from psychotherapy. Because of strong feelings of fears toward religion, fear that the therapist will insert his or her values into therapy, a simplistic view of religious experiences, and simplistic understanding of religious experience, lack of religious education or reasoning. The level of comfort and level of competence of a therapist working within a religious frame may be determined by his personal history.[8]

Griffith further expounds how God can be used therapeutically with counselees and their families. He suggests that God can be used as the ultimate family member so that the

> God-family relationship can be defined as a public position of the family regarding God or as, the way private relationships between God and various family members affect family functioning. For religious families God may be readily available to reshape conflictual relationships in family therapy.[9]

A case example demonstrates the power of religion in enacting change when dealing with a black counselee with a strong Christian orientation.

> Eubie was a thirty-one-year-old man who was in therapy for spouse abuse. He and his wife were born-again Christians. His wife, Diane, was thirty-one. The couple had three children.
>
> After the last abusive episode, the wife and children moved to a shelter for battered wives. The husband had voluntarily

come into therapy as a step toward reconciliation with his wife.

It took three sessions with him to uncover his affect and finally face his violence toward his wife. In fact he wept with remorse as we went through the cycle that led to the abuse of his wife. The Holy Spirit enabled me to help him because Eubie was a born-again Christian. He believed it was God who had helped him and his wife survive the struggles they faced as a black couple. Eubie had a conscience that could be tapped and thus was able to recognize the inconsistency of his behavior with his Christian values. Finally, he was ready to enter into a "no violence" contract, often used in marriage counseling when violence has occurred between couples. It is a written agreement devised and signed by the couple to cease all physical violence. The offender bears a consequence determined by the couple beforehand. However, I ran into a major roadblock at the next session. Eubie came in adamant about not signing the contract, thinking it unfair since he was the one who had been violent, not his wife. After unsuccessfully dealing with his feelings and distortions, I used the strength of this family—namely religion. I changed the contract title to "Covenant," and told Eubie it would be between him and his wife, with God as witness. To this interpretation he readily agreed and the therapy was able to continue.

Finally, many blacks come from family backgrounds where witchcraft, root working, and mysticism were accepted practices. These occultish beliefs may be mixed with their Christian faith. Counselors patiently and biblically will have to challenge these ideas.

In summary, Christian counseling requires awareness of ethnic issues, gender issues, and environmental issues. But counselors must also be mindful that African-Americans as spiritual beings are often incurably religious. Thus, the empowering of the Holy Spirit and God's infallible Word remain the best means of connecting with African-American people.

There is no better example of this fact than Philip's experience with the Ethiopian eunuch. Philip faced all of the issues, but was able to transcend each one because he yielded to the Spirit and allowed himself to be an instrument through whom the love, life, and light of God were channeled. Philip was able to achieve this in spite of obvious ethnic, socioeconomic, and religious differences between the eunuch and himself. He demonstrated that a Christian can overcome such differences and reach people who are dissimilar. Philip also developed a relationship with the eunuch that exemplified the principles of an effectual counseling process. These principles are the subject of Part II.

NOTES

[1]Staples, *Black Masculinity*, 31.

[2]William H. Grier and Price M. Cobbs, *The Jesus Bag* (New York: McGraw-Hill, 1971), 155.

[3]William Harrison Pipes, "Old Time Religion Benches Can't Say Amen," *Black Families*, ed., Harriette Pipers-McAdoo, (Beverly Hills: Sage Publications, 1981).

[4]William L. Banks, *The Black Church in the U.S.: Its Origin Growth Contribution and Outlook* (Chicago: Moody, 1972), 98.

[5]Ibid.

[6]S. Bruce Narramore, *No Condemnation: Rethinking Guilt Motivation in Counseling, Preaching and Parenting* (Grand Rapids: Zondervan, 1984), 259.

[7]Quentin Q. Hyder, *The Christian's Handbook of Psychiatry* (Old Tappan: Spire, 1973), 127.

[8]James L. Griffith, "Employing the God-Family Relationship in Therapy With Religious Families," *Family Process* 25 (December 1986): 614–17.

[9]Ibid.

Part II

THE COUNSELING PROCESS AND BLACK COUNSELEES: TEN BIBLICAL PRINCIPLES

8

DIRECTIVE ENGAGING

"He arose and went" (Acts 8:27)

The first of Philip's activities is found in verse 26: "And the angel of the Lord spake unto Philip, saying, Arise, and go toward the south unto the way that goeth down from Jerusalem unto Gaza, which is desert." This particular activity has been labeled "directive engaging." *Engaging* means initiating a counselee to the counseling process. *Directive* means the leading of God as the act of engaging. Philip was directed by the angel of the Lord to pursue his mission with the eunuch.

In like manner, all Christian counselors must be sensitive to God's leading as they enter into a relationship with black counselees. This discussion will center on the role of God's leading in the engaging process, difficulties engaging blacks, methods of engaging, and some suggestions for white counselors. If the counseling process does not begin correctly, there is a strong possibility that it may not proceed or terminate well. Directive engaging helps assure a good start.

GOD'S LEADING IN ENGAGING

Philip arose and went to the Gaza desert to meet the eunuch because those were the specific instructions given him by the angel of the Lord. So one could say his first meeting with the eunuch was staged by God.

Likewise, we who are counselors must be in tune to God's leading with the Word and prayer. We may not know how to engage counselees at the first meeting, but our omniscient God knows how. For those of us who take the opportunity to acknowledge him in all our ways, he will direct our paths (Proverbs 3:6).

For a number of reasons, God's leading is imperative in the engaging process. First of all, it enables the counselor to engage the counselee at the right time and place. Philip was given specific guidance from God regarding time and place. Timing is crucial when engaging blacks. If counselors do not seize the right opportunity, prospective counselees will pull back from therapy. Since no one can ever be sure when the right timing is, reliance on God's direction is a must. This is especially significant because blacks are more prone than whites to be suspicious of counseling and are less enthusiastic about its merits. If counselors do not respect timing and try to engage too soon or too late, they may well jeopardize their chances for success. We are reminded in Proverbs 15:23, "a word spoken in due season, how good is it!" To be able to speak the right word in due season involves timing—and timing involves God's leading.

Second, God's direction is indispensable because blacks frequently have a cultural predisposition not to disclose their problems in counseling. Therefore, it is difficult simply to judge them on the basis of what is observed in the sessions. Counselors led by God often discern underlying problems even when the counselee is not self-disclosing. This was a divine trait found in Jesus. He was so in touch with his Father that the Bible says of his dealing with people, "He knew their thoughts." The counselors God directs are able to see into the window of people's spirits, thoughts, and emotions as they become transparent before God. As the Psalmist exclaimed, "If I say, Surely the darkness shall cover me; even the night shall be light about me. Yea . . . the darkness and the light are both alike to thee" (Psalm 139:11, 12).

Finally, God's direction is integral to engaging because it serves to counter anxiety. Engaging can be an anxious experience and counselees detect this anxiety in their counselors. However, when counselors are guided by God, pressure and anxiety are minimized because they are following God's plan based on God's will, and depend on God's results. If counselors are leaning on their own understanding, they have good reason to be anxious. If they are being steered by God, the responsibility for success lies with God, not counselors. So regardless of what happens we counselors rest assured because we are obeying God's agenda.

In summary, there are two necessary tasks in the directive engaging process—to identify God's leading and to obey it. Without the performance of both tasks, the process will not succeed.

Directive engaging is critical in relating to black counselees, who at times are hard to reach. A look at these difficulties may help facilitate this operation.

DIFFICULTIES ENGAGING BLACK COUNSELEES

Obstructions counselors may encounter in engaging minorities are paranoia, resistance, inconsistency, and expectations. Regarding paranoia, Cobbs and Grier maintain that blacks are suspicious of their environment, which is necessary for survival. They must be vigilant and alert to the dangers from white citizens.[1] Counselees may enter therapy either intimidated or be intimidating in a session, particularly if a white Christian is the counselor.

On the matter of resistance, counselors should note the various ways in which black counselees may resist them: nondisclosure of information; false disclosure of information; chronic lateness for appointments; missing appointments; getting angry at the counselor; and accusing white counselors of racism. Resistance may also take the following forms: dominating sessions with obsessive talking; excessive jesting; nodding off to sleep; creating distractions; failing to pay for counseling; forgetting assignments; creating an argument or fight in the office.

With regard to inconsistency, blacks may miss appointments not only from resistance, but as a response to stress and legitimate economic pressures. Child care may not be available to accommodate the times of counseling. In dysfunctional black families, crises may constantly arise that preclude consistent attendance. Korchin noted the results of a study of nearly fourteen thousand clients seen in seventeen community mental health centers in the greater Seattle area. Over a three-year period he found about half of all ethnic-group clients failed to return after one session—a significantly higher proportion than white clients. Even though economic status was controlled statistically, the difference between minority and white clients in non-return rates remained statistically significant.[2]

Counselors may find themselves at odds with black counselees on the issue of expectations. Often the expectations for therapy among minority counselees do not mesh with those of white therapists. When those expectations are disappointed, minority counselees are less likely to continue counseling. They want and need more directive intervention, explicit advice, financial counseling, or vocational help than is offered in traditional therapy.[3] In response to these factors, Christian counselors should take the necessary steps to make counseling relevant to the needs of counselees.

Finally, race need not be a deterrent to therapy since white Christians can engage blacks as well as and in some cases better than black Christian counselors, provided they observe a few simple guidelines.

SUGGESTIONS FOR WHITE CHRISTIAN COUNSELORS

One question emerges as a cross-cultural concern in counseling African-Americans: can white therapists effectively counsel blacks? The answer is a conditional yes. It must be remembered that when the Lord directed Philip to engage the Ethiopian eunuch, he surely knew Philip was not black. The evangelist demonstrates that a white person can reach a black person. However, there are a few rules white Christian counselors should follow.

First of all, white Christian counselors must avoid a condescending or patronizing attitude toward African-Americans. This is the old white missionary syndrome that treats African-Americans as pitiful ebony people who need the help of civilized Caucasians. Since blacks are an intuitive people, they pick up on this attitude and respond with outrage, if not black rage. Black counselees need to be treated as equals but different. They need to be given the same deference, respect, and honor accorded white counselees. This is particularly true of the black male. If he can be successfully engaged in a couple of sessions, the odds of therapy continuing and succeeding are greatly increased. Showing him respect and honor will be a major, positive step in the direction of achieving this end. White Christian counselors must be natural, empathic, warm, attentive, patient, and caring. In other words, the same therapeutic style must be used as with any other counselee.

Second, nonminority counselors must understand that blacks may bring experiences different from the counselors' upbringing. The use of language or humor may be very different. Thus, white Christian counselors must be students as well as instructors. For there is a rich learning experience African-Americans offer if counselors are willing to learn. Moreover, white counselors need to be open to the Holy Spirit's challenging their prejudices, myths, and stereotypes. A new appreciation of and new information about their black brothers and sisters will emerge.

Third, white Christians must utilize religion as a major strength in black families, especially Christian black families. Black families may experience a different kind of worship, but it is still one Lord, one faith, and one baptism we all share (Ephesians 4:5). Black people, like white people, are spirit beings, and the Christian faith helps the souls of white counselors touch the souls of black counselees.

Fourth, it is incumbent upon white counselors to be honest about what they may not understand about black people. White counselors must inquire about that which may seem novel or idiosyncratic. African-Americans treasure honesty in white counselors because, as a people, we have often been deceived by the larger society.

Finally, white Christian counselors must look for the commonalities of human experience in black counselees. While it is true that there are cultural and ethnic differences, it is also true that in many ways we are all very much alike. White counselors must tap the well of their own experience and, where relevant, connect with the experiences of black counselees.

Whether counselors are black or white, they must master the art of engaging. It begins the moment counselors contact counselees to set up the first appointment. Engagement is communicated in voice tone and general mood. And it is communicated at the first session through the manner in which counselees are greeted, in body language and eye contact, as well as in the first statement or question of the session. Counselees receive some kind of message regarding the engagement of counselors. Therefore, counselors should strive to make this process an active one. Remember that it was Philip who pursued the eunuch. Bruce Narramore gives an example of the aim of engaging. He says, "A therapist must develop a therapeutic relationship which models self-acceptance, non-punitiveness, and authenticity."[4] This is the first step in an effective relationship with black counselees and the critical precursor to the process of affective joining.

NOTES

[1]Grier and Cobbs, *Black Rage*, 20–30.
[2]Sheldon J. Korchin, "Clinical Psychology and Minority Problems," *American Psychologist* (March 1980).
[3]Ibid., 262.
[4]Narramore, 259.

9

AFFECTIVE JOINING

"Then the Spirit said unto Philip, Go near, and join thyself to this chariot" (Acts 8:29)

The second principle in the counseling process I want to discuss is affective joining. This principle is reflected in Acts 8:29 when the Spirit instructed Philip to join himself to the Ethiopian's chariot. This joining is more than physical—it is affective, an emotional juncture. Joining is the connectedness, the rapport between counselor and counselee. It is the formation of the therapeutic alliance. Here again we see the necessity of God's leading through his Holy Spirit. It was the Spirit who motivated Philip to join with the Ethiopian. As in directive engaging, it is the Spirit who prompts and enables us as counselors to join with counselees. The onus was on Philip, not the eunuch, to initiate the joining. We cannot rely on counselees, who are understandably apprehensive, anxious, and emotionally spent, to make the effort, although they certainly have an important part in the process. To succeed in making the transition in joining, counselors must respect the Ethiopian's chariot and explore the appropriate method for entering it.

RESPECTING THE ETHIOPIAN'S CHARIOT

It is clear from our study of Acts chapter eight, that Philip respected the eunuch and his chariot. He came close to the vehicle but did not enter it impulsively or impetuously. Nor did he force his way in.

The Ethiopian's chariot is a symbol that embodied what the eunuch was about. It represented his space, his world, and his journey as a person. Similarly, all black people who come to counseling bring chariots with them—an emotional vehicle carrying unseen mental space, an inner world, a personal journey. Each rider, chariot, and journey is different. Every Ethiopian brings a chariot into the counseling session. In Christian counseling the chariot is often not respected, and counselors try to enter too soon, too hastily, too abruptly, or too forcefully, provoking black counselees to defend their chariots or ride away in retreat. Christian counselors must be patient and wait for the right moment for the joining process to occur, all the while continuing to engage counselees.

When is the right moment for joining to happen? In the scriptural text it was the moment the eunuch invited Philip to enter the chariot. We read, "He desired Philip that he would come up and sit with him" (Acts 8:31). Counselors will know the right moment to join because counselees will invite them. It will be a message or a signal—a verbal cue, such as an amicable conversation with self-disclosing information, or a nonverbal cue, such as a congenial smile. In some manner counselees will signal that the time is right for counselors to bond with them. An example of joining is illustrated in the following case:

> Dionne and Wade are a young black couple in their early thirties. They have been married four years and have one son, two years old. Dionne is pregnant with their second child. Wade works as a counterman at a seafood restaurant and Dionne is a homemaker.

> The couple was experiencing heightened tension, heated arguments, and volatile domestic quarrels. Dionne accused Wade of a number of extramarital affairs. In the first session I noted that Wade was passive-dependent and Dionne active-aggressive. Dionne did most of the talking while Wade remained silent and aloof. I detected a reluctance on Wade's part to be in counseling. He confirmed my suspicion, indicating that he came only because Dionne badgered him into coming. He did not like telling his problems to strangers and did not want to disclose much of his personal life. It was apparent that Dionne was more committed to the therapy

than Wade. If the conjoint sessions were to continue, I knew I would need to engage him more than Dionne and join with him quickly. This involved focusing more attention on Wade and less on Dionne without making her feel neglected. I had to assess Dionne's ability to handle this situation.

I concluded that I could take the risk with her. I then spent most of the session endeavoring to engage Wade through use of disarming statements like "I know it must be difficult to be here. I would be reluctant to spill my guts to a stranger." Second, I used Wade's experience with seafood as a means to connect with him, and we discussed his favorite seafood dishes.

The third way I engaged the client was with humor. After about a half hour I noticed Wade's body posture changing. He stopped slouching and sat in a more attentive position, made eye contact with me instead of looking away, and assumed a more open disposition in general. I had intermittent discussion with Dionne at various intervals to keep her interested and to let her know she was not being ignored. The moment of joining came when Wade, who had been relatively rigid, aloof, and closed, smiled and laughed as I joked about a hilarious experience I once had with a seafood dinner. Wade's smile, laughter, and body posture were my invitation into the chariot.

The next step was to engender conversation. At home Dionne dominated conversations, tended to be critical, and rarely gave Wade an opportunity to talk. I changed that pattern by asking Wade for his version of the problem. I asked for clarification and qualification, questions that demonstrated a listening ear without criticism or judgment. At the end of the session, the man who said he would not talk to a stranger amazed himself and his wife with the amount of information he had disclosed. I helped Wade identify why he felt comfortable talking to me and not his wife. As a result Wade and Dionne contracted for several sessions.

This case indicates the variety of ways a counselor can join with a counselee. Sometimes this may require some exploration and experimentation in the session until the counselor finds what works. Regardless of the method, counselors will be assured of its success if aware of God's direction.

METHODS OF JOINING

In the last case example I used a number of methods to join with the husband. One method was humor. African-Americans are a warm, colorful people who enjoy laughter and mirth. Humor is a good way to join with them. The Scriptures tell us that "a merry heart doeth good like a medicine" (Proverbs 17:22); "a merry heart maketh a cheerful countenance" (Proverbs 15:13); and "a merry heart hath a continual feast" (Proverbs 15:15). There is also "a time to laugh" (Ecclesiastes 3:4). However, counselors should recognize cultural differences in humor. Counselors may laugh at something counselees find quite offensive. One way to evoke laughter is for therapists to laugh at themselves and to demonstrate that they can handle others laughing with them. Using the self in humor makes people feel more comfortable in therapy. Humor defuses tension, loosens rigid posture, relieves anxiety, and fosters hope. Meier, Minirth, and Wichern state that humor is a quality that counselors should have—its power should not be minimized.[1]

Recognizing that counselees are experts in certain areas is another way counselors can join. When clients come to counseling they often put counselors in a powerful position by giving up power themselves. Counselors can return this power by encouraging counselees to share information in areas where they are the experts. Often a good place to start is the counselee's vocation. But for those who are unemployed, exploring some other activity or hobby can serve just as well.

The use of disarming, empathic statements is another way for counselors to join with counselees. Statements such as: "I can understand why you might feel that way" or "I can see that you are very concerned about this" conveys to counselees their right to have feelings. It removes the presumption of judgment on the part of the counselor and creates an environment conducive to sharing.

Discussing the Christian faith in counseling sessions is a means of engaging—the same can be said of its usefulness in joining. Philip was able to enter the chariot because the Ethiopian was a religious man. He had a spiritual need that prompted an invitation to Philip to come into the chariot. Engaging and joining with counselees is what Gary Collins calls Stage I in therapy. Counselors seek to establish a rapport with counselees by communicating warm, accepting, uncritical attitudes to help counselees overcome initial fears.[2] A major skill utilized in the case example about joining was active listening on the part of the counselor. Without active listening, joining will not occur and the counseling process will also suffer. Active listening is a basic, primary skill in counseling.

NOTES

[1]Paul D. Meier, Frank B. Minirth, and Frank Wichern, *Introduction to Psychology: Christian Perspectives and Application* (Grand Rapids: Baker, 1982), 297.

[2]Collins, *Christian Counseling*, 171–79.

10

ACTIVE LISTENING

**"Philip ran thither to him, and heard him read the
prophet Esaias" (Acts 8:30)**

In Acts 8:30 Philip heard the eunuch read. Philip demonstrated that he was an active listener. Counselors must also be active listeners. The Bible emphasizes the role of active listening. We are told to be "swift to hear, slow to speak" (James 1:19), and that a "wise man will hear, and will increase learning" (Proverbs 1:5).

If we are truly as wise as we think we are, our wisdom will be reflected in how well we hear our counselees and learn from them. One of the eight qualities of a good Christian counselor mentioned by Meier, Minirth, and Wichern is the practice of good listening skills.[1] Guldseth suggests that listening allows counselees to express their feelings and experience a catharsis through the use of words. This relieves tension and anxiety, and ventilates conflict.[2] Furthermore, counselors must listen to make assessments, gather data, determine affect and feelings, demonstrate empathy, and interpret use of language.

LISTENING AS A MEANS OF ASSESSING
AND GATHERING DATA

By listening to the Ethiopian eunuch, Philip assessed his need. He heard him read Isaiah and understood the Ethiopian's problem. This gave Philip a basis for intervention and wisdom to know what question to ask.

Listening is crucial in assessing and diagnosing problems.

The Word of God says, "Out of the abundance of the heart the mouth speaketh" (Matthew 12:34). If we will let counselees talk long enough, sooner or later the problems, conflicts, and concerns of their hearts are going to be revealed. Errors in assessment sometimes stem from counselors' failure to listen properly. Important details of a problem, vital information about counselees' families and personal life may be missed. In addition, failure to listen actively also leads to "counselor's folly," described in Proverbs 18:13: "He that answereth a matter before he heareth it, it is folly and shame unto him." We may find ourselves in the embarrassing situation of having prematurely given solutions when we haven't heard the problems. Such an experience during counseling may be discouraging to blacks and leave lasting negative impressions for any future counseling.

LISTENING FOR AFFECT AND FEELING

Active listening enables us to hear the moods, feelings, and emotions behind the content of what is being said. It is not only what counselees say but how they say it. We must listen for anger, hurt, fear, loneliness, anxiety, resentment, bitterness, guilt, and shame. Listening for feeling involves more than the use of one's ears, it also involves the use of one's spiritual gut. Since feelings are usually layered, one must listen for the feeling behind the feeling. The following case demonstrates this point.

> Allen was a twenty-two-year-old black male and a born-again Christian. His fiancée, Vinnie, was a twenty-four-year-old and born again. They came to me for premarital counseling. Allen had completed his degree at a prestigious school of business and worked for a firm in a large city. Vinnie worked as an accountant at a local bank.

> As part of the premarital session I chose to use a genogram (an emotional family tree) to look at some of the family scripts the couple might take into their marriage. I began with Allen. He began to get emotional midway through the session when family interactions over the generations appeared, especially when we discussed his nuclear family.

Allen revealed that his parents never seemed to approve of him no matter what he did. His mother in particular never really gave him compliments. His father was also critical and not very engaging. The more Allen talked, the more his voice quivered. I stopped and inquired what Allen was feeling. He said he was feeling anger. However, I detected that behind the anger were feelings of hurt over this lack of appreciation. The anger was a layer over the hurt. Allen thought for a second and became teary-eyed as he remarked that he was deeply hurt by his parents. I began to show Allen how his parents were reared in homes where neither had love. Allen's mother was born out of wedlock and was often reminded of this throughout her life. Allen saw that his father also was born out of wedlock. Once he saw generational patterns and how his parents were victims too, we could discuss forgiving them even as Christ had forgiven them. Allen accepted this and was ready to move on.

Black men commonly use anger to hide their hurt, and black women use hurt to mask their anger. In either case, if not confronted, these emotions may become hate. Of the relationship between anger and hate, Dr. Cecil Osborne states: "Anger and hate are radically different emotions. Hate is concealed rage. It is anger gone vicious a murderous ongoing feud."[3] Anyone who hates his brother is a murderer, declares the Bible (1 John 3:15).

Osborne goes on to explain why it is important for such feelings to be discharged. He says of hatred: "It is destructive to the hater whose organism, mentally, emotionally and chemically is disturbed."[4]

LISTENING TO DEMONSTRATE EMPATHY

Listening communicates empathy. For many blacks in counseling, listening may prove to be therapy enough. African-Americans commonly feel that no one listens and empathizes with their plight. Counselors will not be able to right all the wrongs done to their black clientele nor remove the misfortunes that befall them. But with the compassion of Christ counselors demonstrate through active listening that they are at least willing to hear the pain their counselees experience.

LISTENING FOR MEANING AND USE OF LANGUAGE

Language is a two-edged sword. Without it, our ability to understand each other is greatly hampered. Yet even when we use language, messages somehow still get mixed up. For this reason active listening is important. Language use differs from person to person, and interpreting messages may not be so simple a task. Many factors affect our use of language: education level, culture, family, gender, values, and moods. So counselors must not make assumptions, but listen to how black counselees use language. When counselees use words like love, hate, fight, relationship, marriage, sex, and even God, do they mean what we think they mean? Low-income blacks may have problems communicating. Their use of language may not be the same as blacks in higher-income brackets. Poorer blacks may speak more colloquially, use "black English" ("He done gone on now," or "I done cooked that some-n-teat"). Young blacks may employ street slang. We need to listen closely to how they use language and for the meaning they attach to their words. Active listening sets the stage for the fourth principle in the counseling process—explorative questioning. When a counselee speaks and a counselor listens, issues come up, thoughts are stimulated, hypotheses develop, hunches are made, and meaning is assigned. Then the counseling process requires exploration through further questioning.

NOTES

[1]Meier, et al, *Introduction to Psychology*, 297.

[2]G. J. Guldseth, *Emotional Ills and the Christian*, (Plainfield: Logos, 1969), 53–55.

[3]Cecil G. Osborne, *Understanding Your Past: The Key to the Future*, (Waco: Word, 1980), 5–100.

[4]Ibid., 168.

11

EXPLORATIVE QUESTIONING

"Understandest thou what thou readest?" (Acts 8:30)

Upon hearing the eunuch read, Philip posed the explorative question, "Understandest thou what thou readest?" Let's speculate how Philip may have used this question. It was a strategic question designed to explore a number of factors. It could have been used as a test of the eunuch's comprehension; a way to assess the eunuch's readiness to receive help from a non-Ethiopian; an indirect way of engaging the eunuch; a way to determine the eunuch's ability to respond to a question; a hypothesis about what Philip perceived as his need; and, finally, a way for Philip to introduce himself. The question could have served any one of these purposes, a combination of purposes, or all of them. We are left to speculate and conjecture, since we cannot read Philip's thoughts.

The point is that Philip made timely use of an explorative question that elicited a response. It does not necessarily matter what kind of response one gets. Even if there is no response at all, valuable information is revealed to skilled counselors. Counselors must be skilled at explorative questioning. They must also know what precautions to take when using explorative query with black counselees.

USE OF QUESTIONS

As we have seen, questions may be used for several reasons. Questions may be used to elicit more information.

Since black counselees tend to self-disclose less, counselors may have to pursue more information by asking questions such as "Can you give an example?" or "What else can you tell me about that?" or "Can you say more?"

Questions may also be used to clarify information such as "What do you mean by that?" or "Is this what you're saying?" Such questions enable counselees to give more detail or affirm whether an interpretation is accurate.

Stimulation of the thinking process is yet another way questions may be utilized. Questions such as "What did that mean to you?" or "How do you think that happens?" or even "Why do you think you do that?" are ways to get counselees to reflect on their behavior and actions.

Questions confirm perceptions and hypotheses: "It would appear from your actions that you are angry. Is that correct?" or "Are you upset about this?" or "Are you anxious?"

These are not the only ways questions are used. Friedman, in *Generation to Generation*, states:

> An approach that primarily asks questions, sometimes consciously naïve, also keeps the counselor out of the dependency-encouraging expert position that fosters giving wise advice. Furthermore, it is hard to give answers if you are asking the questions. Some questions are designed to bring out the symmetry in the relationship. Others are playfully designed to tone down emotionality so that the partners can hear and the counselor retain objectivity. Some have a paradoxical intent, designed to challenge the thoughts of one of the partners by taking his or her thinking to its ultimate extreme.[1]

Good explorative questioning will involve who, what, where, when, why, and how. They must be asked in a balanced, timely fashion. Explorative questioning is used in the following case excerpt:

> Martha is a twenty-four-year-old black woman who is a born-again believer. She is married to Andy, a police officer, age twenty-five, and has a little boy two years old. Martha is employed as a social worker in an AIDS treatment clinic.

She came to counseling because her husband had a number of affairs and told her that he did not love her. The couple has been married for four years and had problems from the beginning. Several women called the house, and Martha found pictures of her husband with another woman. She left Andy because of these incidents. After a while, Martha returned to Andy only to hear him admit that he is still involved in the affair. Martha felt caught in a relationship she wanted to leave, but she does not believe in divorce. She felt hopeless about changing Andy. The following is a session in which I used questions to explore issues.

Therapist:	I hear you say that you feel caught in the relationship. Can you say more about that?
Martha:	(Thinking) I mean I feel as though I am caught in a marriage with a man who isn't saved, who doesn't love me, and who is going with other women.
Therapist:	You sound hurt and angry. Is that what you're feeling now?
Martha:	(Eyes tearing) Yes, I am.
Therapist:	I can see that this is painful for you. (Pause) Is your anger directed at just Andy, or is it directed at yourself, too?
Martha:	(Pause to reflect) I guess I'm angry at Andy for taking me through these changes. I'm angry at myself for getting into the situation, and I'm angry at God for allowing me to be in the situation.
Therapist:	Who are you most angry with?
Martha:	(Pause to reflect) I guess with myself (getting teary-eyed).
Therapist:	What are you thinking and feeling now?
Martha:	(Starting to cry) That I'm a failure. I failed God and myself.

Through a series of explorative questions, I was able to bring Martha to admit her underlying feelings of inadequacy. Notwithstanding, questions need to be asked in such a way as not to turn off black counselees. Certain cautions need to be observed.

CAUTIONS IN QUESTIONING BLACK COUNSELEES

Counselors must use the following guidelines when asking questions of black counselees:

Do not ask very personal questions until sufficient engaging and joining has occurred.

Be willing to be self-disclosing concerning the questions you want answered.

Let counselees know that they do not have to answer any questions. But communicate to them that willingness makes counseling more effective.

Ask open ended questions.

Begin with safe, nonthreatening questions, and gradually build up to more difficult ones.

Since blacks are often more comfortable with the present, try to ask here-and-now questions.

Demonstrate appreciation, support, and empathy when answers are offered.

Assess counselees' readiness before asking very personal or sensitive questions.

Monitor body language and behavioral reactions.

Let counselees know the purpose of the questions.

Be simple, clear, and specific in eliciting information.

Be sensitive to the Spirit's leading about the right timing of questions.

These guidelines will make the explorative questioning process easier and better prepare counselors to gain insight.

NOTE

[1]Edwin H. Friedman, *Generation to Generation: Family Process in Church and Synagogue* (New York: Guildford, 1985), 72.

12

CORRELATIVE BEGINNING

"Philip opened his mouth, and began at the same scripture" (Acts 8:35)

Philip's encounter with the eunuch illustrates the sixth principle in the counseling process—the correlative beginning. This principle of starting an intervention at a point where the client is fixated, stuck or enmeshed in a problem is evident from Acts 8:35—"Philip opened his mouth, and began at the same scripture." In other words, he recognized where the eunuch was stuck in his reading of Isaiah. Philip assessed the eunuch's level of understanding and began there.

After counselors obtain sufficient information through explorative questioning, they must determine where individuals or couples are stuck. If interventions are not correlated to the level of counselees' understanding, counselors interventions may preclude the finding of solutions. There are two steps in correlative beginning. The first step is to discern "stuckness." The next step is to select an intervention congruent with counselee's affective and cognitive levels.

DISCERNING HOW BLACK COUNSELEES GET STUCK

The process of discerning how black counselees get stuck is not different from discerning how non-black counselees get stuck during the counseling process. Counselees who avoid a certain issue or subject, or who cannot alter their perception of a problem to consider an alternative solution are stuck in their journey toward healing. Other signs of counselees getting stuck are lack of empathy with their partners; inability to see their own contributions to problems; unwillingness to change; chronic failure to do therapeutic assignments; and continual sabotage of the counseling process. Therefore, counselors must be alert to redundant behavioral, intrapsychic, and systemic patterns that indicate counselees are stuck. The following case illustrates how black counselees get stuck:

> Ronald was thirty-one years old. He came to counseling with his wife, Louise, concerning an extramarital affair he had. Louise had left because of Ronald's last affair and was now living with parents. Both Ronald and Louise were born-again believers. Ronald began individual therapy to see how he might be reconciled with his wife.

Counselor:	The last time we met you indicated that you wanted to see what you could do to be reconciled with your wife. Apparently what you have been doing has not been successful.
Ronald:	I'm not the problem. She is the problem. Everything will be all right if she will come clean, admit her sin, and conform to God's Word to be submissive to her husband.
Counselor:	So then, am I hearing you say that you don't want to work on your part of the reconciliation?
Ronald:	I'm doing that by being here.
Counselor:	I would agree with you. But I understood you to say that you wanted to see what you could do—that you wanted to work on your part in these sessions since she isn't here.
Ronald:	She was wrong to leave me. She was out of the will of God.
Counselor:	What is your part in the problem? Or do you believe that one person is totally at fault in this relationship?
Ronald:	It's not on me. It's on her, man.
Counselor:	You said you know the Scriptures well. It says in Ephesians for husbands to love their wives as Christ loved the church. Do you feel you have achieved this completely?

Ronald: I can't love her unless she submits to my authority and admits her sin.

As the counselor, I saw that Ronald was stuck and could not see his own fault in the relationship with his wife. I had to dispense with trying to get him to work on his behavioral changes. Instead, I dealt with the intrapsychic and spiritual defenses that blocked him from acknowledging his own guilt and pain. So I took a self-disclosing approach. I revealed some of my own failures in my endeavors to love my wife within the context of Ephesians 5.

Then I began to identify Ronald's pain under the block, and empathized with that pain. I gently confronted Ronald on some of his one-sided, distorted views of Scripture regarding being head of the home, but avoided a debate so as not to get into a power struggle. I sought to increase Ronald's self-esteem through praise and appreciation, which allowed him to feel safe and lower some of his defenses. Most importantly, I became conscious of abandoning myself to the Holy Spirit's leading.

By the end of the session, Ronald was able to admit his pain and that he had some part in the failure of his marriage. Ronald said that he would try to work on some of his own issues in individual therapy.

This case illustrates the principle of Proverbs 18:19—"A brother offended is harder to be won than a strong city: and their contentions are like the bars of a castle." Ronald was offended by his wife's abandoning him, and his defense mechanisms were well fortified. This is the image of being stuck. If counselors do not recognize this phenomenon, they are likely to find themselves caught in a vicious cycle in which little is accomplished. When counseling sessions are going nowhere and when we, as counselors, feel powerless in our relationships with counselees, the therapeutic process is stuck. Once counselors acknowledge this phenomenon, they need to select a point of intervention to break the impasse.

SELECTING INTERVENTIVE STARTING POINTS

The eunuch was stuck at the point of his failure to understand Isaiah 53:7–8. When Philip intervened, he did not start at what preceded these verses or at what followed them. But he responded by beginning "at the same Scripture." Counselors must intervene at the specific points of counselees' needs. For blacks, these needs often are anger at parents, spouses, white society, and God. Other stuck places include economic concerns, guilt, self-hatred, insecurity, depression, negativism, paranoia, and dependency.

Since all stuck places are rooted in man's sinful Adamic nature, the first step in the process (for those black counselees who have not done so) is to receive Christ as Lord and Savior. This means that counselors must be aware of opportunities to introduce counselees to the Savior.

13

INTEGRATIVE WITNESSING

"Preached unto him Jesus" (Acts 8:35)

The Scriptures tell us that Philip "preached unto him Jesus." The word *preached* in New Testament Greek is *euēnggelizato*. It means to announce the good news or to bring glad tidings It does not refer to a vocal, passionate sermon. Philip was in the chariot with the eunuch; there was no need to shout at him.

Similarly, Christian counselors need to integrate witnessing into therapy as a simple presentation of the gospel message. As counselors, we need not be reluctant to witness because the Good News is the most effective therapy that we can offer counselees. Guldseth states: "The living Word and written Word of God is the profoundest and most effective therapeutic agency for the treatment of emotional ills."[1]

The issue of evangelism in Christian counseling is a controversial subject, however, and it is here that pastoral counselors have the greatest latitude. Counselors who believe that witnessing should be part of therapy should consider the uses that follow, proposed by Luciano and Bess L'Abate.

FIVE USES OF THE GOSPEL

The L'Abates, who are family counselors, suggest that there are five positive uses of religion in therapy. A good presentation of the Gospel through integrative witnessing meets the criteria for all five uses.[2]

The first use, the L'Abates explain, is that religion can help counselees experience comfort in themselves. The message of Christ serves this function well. Since discomfort in oneself is a by-product of separation from God, through Christ we have peace with God out of which comes a comfort within oneself.

Second, the L'Abates maintain that the purpose of religion is to give meaning to oneself. When received by an individual, the Gospel message results in a change of relationship into that of children of God (John 1:12). The implications of this for experiencing meaning in life are marvelously reassuring.

The third use of religion is to help one make changes in one's life. The Scriptures state that in Christ we are "new creature[s]: old things are passed away; . . . all things are become new" (2 Corinthians 5:17). God's message is the only medium containing the power to transform our old lifestyle into a new one. This is why Paul refers to it as "the power of God unto salvation" (Romans 1:16).

Getting counselees to assume responsibility for their actions is the fourth role of religion in therapy, and the Good News fulfills this function. The saving Word of God, once received, gives one a new sensitivity to spiritual things, especially a new morality. It motivates us to relate to our neighbors in ways that depart from the norm. It calls upon us to be doers of the word and not hearers only (James 1:22). It challenges us to judge ourselves (1 Corinthians 11:31). It reveals God's standard of righteousness and conduct (Romans 1:17). Finally, it gives us a sobering admonition for such conduct by reminding us that "God shall judge the secrets of men by Jesus Christ" (Romans 2:16).

The final role that religion plays is in motivating people to seek help. The Gospel of Christ causes people to reach to God for help. It shows us that we are powerless to free ourselves from sin. Hence, we can only cry as the apostle cried, "O wretched man that I am! who shall deliver me from the body of this death?" (Romans 7:24). Counselees may seek help because they are conscious of their spiritual and human wretchedness. They are searching for someone who can aid them to secure relief from these feelings. It is a serious mistake to allow counselees to think that counselors, in their own strength, can deliver them from their wretchedness. Our role is to direct counselees whose emotional ills have an organic base to the One who is the Great Physician; and for those whose problems have an emotional or spiritual origin to the One who is the Mighty Counselor. Christian clinicians or pastoral counselors who do not allow opportunity for integrative witnessing as part of the counseling process provide insufficient therapy regardless of how successful such therapy may appear. Our counselees come to us assuming that we are wise. If they know we are Christians, they will expect us to be wise in the things of God. That wisdom will not only be demonstrated by what we do as trained clinicians and clergy but also by what we do as competent soul winners. Remember, "he that winneth souls is wise" (Proverbs 11:30).

Nevertheless, Christian counselors must consider a few things when witnessing to African-Americans. Counselors must identify the kind of sinner one is dealing with and determine the approach best suited to that person.

DEALING WITH THE THREE KINDS OF SINNERS

Romans 1–3 discusses three kinds of sinners. Romans 1:18–32 addresses the rational sinner; Romans 2:1–16, the reformed sinner; and Romans 2:17–3:31, the religious sinner.[3] These three types of sinners cut across, race, ethnicity, and culture, and sooner or later appear in the counselor's office.

Compared to whites, black counselees differ only in certain cultural and ethnic features. Rational sinners, who are "vain in their imaginations, and [whose] foolish heart[s are] darkened" (Romans 1:21) and who have sought to extinguish "the true Light, which lighteth every man" (John 1:9), may appear as black males involved in infidelity without any remorse. These men rationalize their behavior.

Or the rational sinner may appear as the intellectual, active in social-action causes, fighting racism and/or sexism. This person may be an admitted atheist who views Christianity as the white man's religion or religion in general as the opiate of the people. Such a person may also come into counseling as the abusive spouse or parent who chronically inflicts pain on a black family member. This person excuses such conduct by rationalizing that the victims receive exactly what they deserve.

Finally, rational sinners may come to counseling as individuals who rebel against external moral restraints on their personal lives. These counselees may be self-centered and use people for their own ends. They are often sociopaths with no respect for life, property, and others' rights. They are haters of God, totally insubordinate to any authority outside of themselves.

When witnessing to the rational sinner, Christian counselors must keep in mind that these people have strong ego defenses that cause them to rationalize and intellectualize away both the existence of God and the destructive effects of their sins. They are described as people who not only do these things "but have pleasure in them that do them" (Romans 1:32).

If counselors are not careful with rational sinners, they will find themselves trapped by mental games such counselees often play. Therapists may find themselves locked in a cycle of philosophical jousting that wastes precious time. This is particularly true when dealing with an intellectual black male. Such a counselee gladly accepts the challenge of ideological debate. It gives his ego great gratification to try and prove believers wrong. Rather than debate him, a more productive strategy for counselors is to join patiently with these individuals, identifying feelings of guilt, anger, hurt, and fear. Thus, a counselee may momentarily become vulnerable to an evangelistic message. In any case, counselors must avoid any temptation to intellectualize. Instead, they must share the clear concise message of the Gospel with an attitude of love and humility, leaving the results to the Holy Spirit.

Still another type of sinner is the reformed sinner (Romans 2:1–16). Although believers in God, these sinners tend to be more cosmopolitan about religion. They are often moral, working-class and middle-class blacks who know they are better than those poor folks in the ghetto. The contrast between reformed sinners and black religious sinners is that the reformed sinner does not necessarily believe in organized religion. They are humanists. They believe in the brotherhood of man and in God as the deity of all religions. Such counselees make statements like "I am serving the Creator by doing my duty to humanity." Therefore, they may belong to the NAACP, the Urban League, Operation PUSH, black fraternities or sororities, community organizations, or minority political caucuses. These counselees tend to be relatively successful African-Americans who look upon God's goodness as a sign of his special favor, not realizing that his goodness is meant to lead them to repentance (Romans 2:4). Counselors must enable such counselees to understand that only through Christ can we be righteous, not through mere altruism.

As for the religious sinner described in Romans 2:17–3:31, counselors have more leverage since this sinner comes to counseling with a consciousness of God. As black counselees, religious sinners are pious church folk, many of whom are not saved but participate in clubs, auxiliaries, and social functions of the church. These counselees gladly tell you that they are children of black ministers, deacons, or other religious luminaries. They "pay their dues and do as they choose." They believe that, based upon their good moral life and general absence of vices, they score brownie points with the Creator.

Another way religious sinners may appear in counseling is as members of the Black Muslims. The Islamic influence on African-Americans is still fairly popular. This is partly due to the appeal of national figures such as Louis Farrakhan, Kareem Abdul Jabbar, and Ahmad Rashad.

When the religious sinner has a Christian view, the counselor can point out how works do not save us; the meaning of the Lord's death, burial, and resurrection; and emphasize that Christ and not religion is the way to God. But with blacks who are part of other religions, Christian counselors need to discern where they are in their religious beliefs. Often blacks are spiritually hungry, but frustrated with the church and so seek out other religions—only to find their frustrations remain. If Christian counselors (especially pastors) access counselees' disappointments with religion, they can explore those disappointments as a route to presenting the message of Christ. With counselees committed to their sect, counselors may present the Gospel as the obvious alternative. In other words, counselors may use a kind of "this is why I believe in Jesus" approach.

Counselees are more open to counselors who show respect for their right to believe differently. In such a case the greater witness is love, respect, and care shown to the nonbeliever in therapy.

The following case demonstrates a witnessing approach with a religious and reformed sinner.

Gary was twenty-nine years old and a teacher in the Philadelphia public school system. Ola was thirty-one years old and a travel agent. The two had come to therapy because of marital and communication problems.

Gary was talking much about divorce. In fact, he gave Ola a year from the time they entered counseling until he left to seek a divorce. Gary felt trapped in the marriage, was bored with the relationship, and wanted to be on his own. I tried a series of interventions that did not work with the couple, including communication-skills training, conflict resolution, family-of-origin work, and contracting. They were both hurting and drained by the situation. They were ready for a witness from me.

Therapist: It would appear that we are at an impasse. It seems the two of you don't really want to work on this relationship. There are too many things blocking you that you don't want to deal with.

Gary: Yeah, I know.

Therapist: What are you feeling, Ola?

Ola: I feel empty, drained, and just dead on the inside.

Therapist: You know one of the things I've wanted to ask you but have been waiting for the right moment is whether or not you are involved in a church or have any kind of religious affiliation.

Ola: I used to go to church when I was little. I was raised in the church and my father was a deacon. And I believe in God.

Therapist: OK, what about you, Gary?

Gary: Well, I'm not into going to any particular church. I do believe in a Creator, but I don't

	knock anybody's religion—whatever they believe is OK with me.
Therapist:	I hear the two of you saying that you believe in God. But let's go one step further. Have you ever thought about receiving Christ as Lord?
Ola:	Yeah. Well, I say my prayers each night and, like I said, I grew up in the church.
Therapist:	Yes, and that certainly is commendable. But, Ola, I'm talking about receiving the person of Christ in your heart and not so much church.
Gary:	(uncomfortable) Well, me and God are cool. He wakes me up every day and he feeds us. I mean we both got good jobs and are in reasonably good health.
Therapist:	You're right. He has blessed you with all those things and yet both of you have admitted that there is something wrong with your relationship, which the two of you, even with the help of a therapist, seem unable to fix. Ola, you mentioned your dead empty feeling on the inside. And you, Gary, agreed that the two of you seem not to be able to get on with the relationship. It may be that God has been showing all this goodness because in his love and patience he was trying to bring you to the place where you could accept his Son. What do you think about that?
Gary:	(reflective) I don't know.
Therapist:	Ola?
Ola:	(tearing) All I know is that I'm tired, and I need my life and marriage to be better, and maybe I do need God in my life. Nothing else seems to work.
Gary:	I'm not ready for religion right now and I don't want to be a hypocrite and say I'm going to do something that I know I'm not.
Therapist:	You may not feel ready, Gary, but God tells you to come now, in the day you hear his voice not to harden your heart. And you know what? The two of you really don't have many

> other options left. I have seen your pain,
> struggles, and frustrations. You are tying to get
> from each other what only God can give you
> unconditionally: love and acceptance, and to
> be at peace with yourself. Christ can give that
> to you if you give him a chance.

The couple did not want to receive Christ at that moment but left in a reflective mood. Yet I felt that I had sown the seed. About two weeks later Ola called to say that she and Gary had been thinking about our discussion during the counseling session. Never before had anyone explained to her how to receive Christ. I replied that she should simply ask God's forgiveness and by faith accept Christ into her heart. She did so over the phone. Gary didn't receive Christ right away, but during a phone call several months later he told me that he, too, had become a Christian and that he and Ola were attending church. While things were not perfect between them, their relationship had definitely improved.

This case illustrates one approach a counselor employed in dealing with a couple of whom one partner was a religious sinner and the other a reformed sinner. The approach is not the only useful one available, but it is the one the counselor was prompted by the Holy Spirit to use to reach this couple for Christ. This case also demonstrates that sometimes it is appropriate that the counselor merely sow a seed for other Christians to water, and God will give the increase in his divine season. If witnessing is to have a part in the counseling process, it has to be included as one of a number of therapy goals. This, then, strongly implies the urgent need to formulate objectives.

NOTES

[1]Guldseth, 53–55.

[2]Luciano L'Abate and Bess L'Abate, *How to Avoid Divorce: Help for Troubled Marriages* (Atlanta: John Knox, 1977), 88–94.

[3]John D. Brooke, *The Five Major Doctrines of the Christian Faith* (Newburgh, Ind: Brooke Ministries, 1982), 81–137.

14

OBJECTIVE PROCEEDING

"As they went on their way" (Acts 8:36)

Philip engaged the eunuch; joined him in the chariot; carefully listened to him; identified the eunuch's need using explorative questions; intervened at the Scripture; and preached Jesus. Together, Philip and the eunuch went on their way (Acts 8:36).

The eighth principle of the counseling process is objective proceeding. Objective proceeding is the planned objectives upon which a relationship will proceed. Too often counseling is either nondirected or one-sidedly directed. Counselors are sometimes so preoccupied with their own agendas that the wishes of counselees are ignored. Counselors abdicate responsibility by letting counselees' goals dominate. Neither one of these positions is appropriate. Counselees and counselors must agree on goals that help them both ride the same chariot in the same direction. But counselors first need to be clear about the goals of biblical counseling.

THE GOALS OF BIBLICAL COUNSELING

Larry Crabb states that Christian counseling should have as its goal the promotion of Christian maturity, helping people enter into a richer experience of worship, and an effective life of service.[1] When dealing with couples, counselors should seek to resolve interpersonal conflicts, help couples disagree or agree constructively, and improve communication; encourage each individual to meet the needs of the respective mate; clarify role relationships; build Christian values in the family; and strengthen the ability of each family member to cope with stress in a healthful manner.[2]

Clyde Narramore suggests that counselors must help counselees express and release strong feelings; accept the fact that adjustments in marriage require time; understand themselves; understand the counseling relationship; understand the roles of a spouse; attain Christian maturity; translate new understanding into appropriate action; feel confident in their ability to improve marriage; and recognize the counselees' efforts to change.[3]

When counseling individuals, Crabb suggests that counselors empathize with painful feelings; identify sinful behavior patterns responsible for negative emotions; uncover the wrong thinking that led to poor behavior; enlighten the individual to biblical thinking about personal needs; and secure a commitment to behavior consistent with truth.[4]

L'Abate states that counselors need to distinguish short-term goals from long-term goals. With short-term goals counselors help counselees obtain symptomatic relief. The long-term goals include improving communication; feeling accepted as individuals; developing flexible assumptions regarding leadership; improving empathy; improving problem-solving abilities; improving sensitivity; decreasing externalization and victimization patterns; and developing a functional balance between individual autonomy and family solidarity. Counselors should aim also to relieve the symptom bearer. That is, spread the blame and focus from the person who has the presenting problem to the larger family system. Usually clients are not totally responsible for their problems.[5]

Collins puts counseling goals and objectives in the context of stages. In stage one, the beginning, counselors have the objective of establishing a rapport with counselees by communicating a warm, accepting attitude. In the second stage, counselors encourage detailed discussion of specific conflict situations and expressions of feelings; raise questions and make comments to stimulate clarification of issues and feelings; and continue to give support and encouragement. In stage three, counselors develop and try tentative solutions. In the final stage, the termination phase, therapy objectives involve helping counselees review progress and assure them of continued availability of therapy.[6]

In addition, I have developed goals and objectives applicable to black Christian counselees. Counselors must encourage and facilitate the spiritual growth of the black family, couples, and individuals; scripturally empower counselees to address the socioeconomic forces that negatively impact them; help them build self-esteem and appreciation of their ethnic identity from a biblical, Afro-centric perspective; enable counselees to alter negative dependency patterns to become more self-reliant and self-sufficient; utilize the intergenerational strengths of the black family as an adjunct to therapy and counseling; enable counselees to express and find more constructive uses for their anger and "black rage"; help them become more individuated and differentiated from their family of origin; help restructure marital and family boundaries; and help alter negative cognitive processes with respect to self, others, and God.

Counselors establish goals and objectives with the intent of helping counselees achieve their goals and objectives. Therefore, setting goals is a means of empowering counselees and returning to them control over their lives. This is why counselors must ascertain early in the counseling process what counselees want to see changed, and work with them to accomplish those aims. After all, it is the Ethiopian's chariot, and he must have a major say in which direction it goes.

GOAL SETTING AS AN EMPOWERING TOOL

Counselors use goal setting in a number of ways to empower counselees. First, goal setting emphasizes that counselees do have choices and can make decisions for themselves. Some African-Americans have difficulty believing that choice is an available option.

Goal setting also gives counselees purpose, something to pursue. This is extremely empowering for blacks who, in many cases, surmise that there is little purpose for them. If motivated to set goals and encouraged to "to do all things through Christ," a new sense of meaning blossoms.

Finally, goal setting provides opportunities to attain short-term victories. Counselees learn how to take problems and break them down into manageable parts. Goal setting prepares the way for therapeutic interventions. Effective biblical counseling is not the result of happenstance or whim. It is that which comes out of good planning procedure, incorporating the expertise of counselors and the concerns of counselees.

NOTES

[1]Lawrence J. Crabb, *Effective Biblical Counseling: A Model for Helping Caring Christians Become Capable Counselors* (Grand Rapids: Zondervan, 1977), 29.

[2]Meier, et al., 308–312.

[3]Clyde M. Narramore, *The Psychology of Counseling* (Grand Rapids: Zondervan, 1960), 184–95.

[4]Crabb, 183.

[5]Luciano L'Abate, Gary Ganahl, and James C. Hanien, *Methods of Family Therapy* (Englewood: Prentice-Hall, 1986), 244.

[6]Collins, 170–79.

15

EFFECTIVE COUNSELING

**"Philip said, If thou believest
with all thine heart" (Acts 8:37)**

There came a point in the journey where the eunuch said, "Here is water; what doth hinder me to be baptized?" (Acts 8:36). At this juncture Philip was able to impart the specifics of what the eunuch needed to do to change his situation. Philip counseled, "If thou believest with all thine heart, thou mayest" (v. 37). There comes a point in our counseling when counselees want to know what they should do to change specific situations and make things better. It is at this point that the counselor's wisdom, experience, knowledge, and expertise is summoned.

Effective biblical counseling has elements similar to secular counseling, but preserves features that make it very different. Biblical counseling accepts Scripture as the final standard of authority. The enabling, indwelling power of the Holy Spirit is critical to biblical counselors in conquering human problems. Furthermore, biblical counseling deals with human beings as whole persons and is based on God's love.[1] Paul Tournier states:

> We need more than a new moral contagion that brings about a change in deep seated attitudes, we need a breath of fresh air, the breath of God's Spirit. No other force in the world can touch a man more deeply in his heart and make him more apt at last at understanding others.[2]

In these ways biblical counseling departs from secular therapy.

ROLES FOR CHRISTIAN COUNSELORS

To do effective biblical counseling requires a repertoire of roles, some of which have been previously discussed. At different times such roles involve empathizing, supporting, accepting, absolving, assessing, leading, teaching, coaching, reflecting, mirroring, revealing, mediating, conciliating, catalyzing, releasing, amplifying, modeling, self-disclosing, challenging, confronting, directing, and reframing. From a biblical perspective several other roles should be added: edifying,[3] witnessing, admonishing, exhorting, praying, comforting, forbearing, reproving, and instructing.

Whatever roles counselors utilize must be done in the context of 1 Corinthians 9:20–22: ". . . unto the Jews I became as a Jew, that I might gain the Jews; to them that are under the law, as under the law, that I might gain them that are under the law; To them that are without law, as without law, (being not without law to God, but under the law to Christ,) that I might gain them that are without law. To the weak became I as weak, that I might gain the weak: I am made all things to all men, that I might by all means save some." This passage captures the sense of the various practices Christian counselors use.

If counselors are inflexible in practicing their roles, their counseling will be myopic and their clientele limited. Moreover, without a wide variety of roles in their repertoire, such counselors risk the possibility of being ineffectual with black counselees, whose transitional patterns of family kinship are not conducive to unilateral interventions.

LEVELS OF BIBLICAL COUNSELING

There are three levels of Christian counseling. Level one consists of problem feelings. At this level counselors help black counselees identify their problem feelings, such as black rage, depression, fear, and anxiety. Counselors encourage them, using a number of roles to help counselees achieve a relationship with God that will result in changed attitudes and feelings.

Level two examines problem behavior. Counselors identify behavior patterns that are counterproductive and need to be changed. Counselors then encourage changes that are in line with biblical behavior.

The third level treats problem thinking. Counselors diagnose distorted cognition and challenge negative thought processes. Counselees are then ready to be enlightened on what the Bible says concerning right thinking.[4]

Biblical counselors must be aware of the stages of the counseling process: the levels of each stage, the goals of each stage, the roles to be used, and the therapeutic principles involved. This is a great deal to try to balance, however, if counselors do not have resources. The most important resource is the Holy Spirit, the Paraclete, who stands alongside Christian therapists to support them. Counselees are themselves resources. They are resources to therapists when they are made accountable for their behavior in the alliance. Otherwise, counselors are put in a position of being totally responsible for the success or failure of counseling. Creating resources in counselees means forming relationships with them that go beyond mere mutuality and goal setting. Counselors create relationships with counselees that are truly conceived in cooperative involving.

NOTES

[1]Meier, et al., 292.

[2]Paul Tournier, *To Understand Each Other* (Atlanta: John Knox, 1974).

[3]Charles P. Barnard and Ramon G. Corrales, *The Theory and Technique of Family Therapy* (Springfield: Charles C. Thomas, 1979), 117–29.

[4]Norman H. Wright, *Marital Counseling: A Biblical Cognitive Approach* (New York: Harper and Row, 1981), 43–60.

16

COOPERATIVE INVOLVING

"And he commanded the chariot to stand still: and they went down both into the water, both Philip and the eunuch; and he baptized him (Acts 8:38)

The crux of successful therapy is the relationship between counselor and counselee. This is true regardless of therapeutic interventions. The therapeutic relationship seems to be the pivotal element in successful counseling. "Cooperative involving" is a mutual agreement between counselor and counselee in the therapy process. The counselor works with the counselee and not for the counselee, thereby avoiding client dependency. When counselors and counselees are actively involved with each other and use a lot of "we language," the experience is more beneficial for both.[1]

Like Philip and the eunuch, Christian counselors and counselees should enter the water together. The chariot ride with explorative questioning, objective proceeding, and effective counseling are all necessary principles of the therapeutic process. Yet there comes a time when the chariot stops so that riders can plunge into the real work. This will not happen unless the chariot is called to a halt by the rider. Since it was the Ethiopian's chariot, he was the one who had to command it to stop.

In like manner, black counselees are the ones who must decide when they want the chariot to stop. It is their responsibility to halt it. They must let counselors know when they are ready to make the transition from simply riding together to really working together, from standing dry in the chariot to standing wet in the river.

Unfortunately, counselors may encounter those who are content to ride the chariot but who do not want to get wet. Such counselees respond to the explorative questions, they receive a witness, they set goals with counselors, and may even give mental assent and acquiescence to advice—but they do not want to get wet. It is so much easier to make the chariot ride, and continue to blame their terrible black parents, their uncaring spouses, impoverished environment, racist white society, Satan, assorted nefarious spirits, and even God. What they are reluctant to do is take the big splash, to choose a river of action and simply plunge in. Yet until they are willing to take action and implement those biblical principles derived from the counseling journey, the chances for genuine growth are nil. There is no cooperative involving unless counselees are willing and committed to do their part. There is, in biblical therapy, a baptism of work in which both counselors and counselees must immerse themselves. Thus, counselors need to remove hindrances to cooperative involvement. These blocks may originate from either counselors or counselees.

COUNSELEE BLOCKS TO COOPERATIVE INVOLVING

Counselee blocks to cooperative involving usually take the form of resistance. Two of these forms have already been mentioned in an earlier chapter—tardiness and absenteeism. Black counselees may resist doing work by not showing up for sessions or by being chronically late for appointments. In addition, other ways this resistance may be evident are deliberately forgetting to do assignments at home or bringing back incompleted and erroneous work. Counselees may fake ignorance to appear much more incompetent than they really are. This is especially true for black counselees who have learned to play the dependence game in order to avoid personal responsibility. They manipulate others to care and nurture them.

Yet another block to cooperative involving is somatizing. Some counselees constantly get sick with psychosomatic illnesses. When counselors observe a constant pattern of illness corresponding to times when serious work is to be done suspicion should be heightened.

Counselees also block serious work and change by projection. Projection occurs when counselees accuse white therapists of racism, black male therapists of bias in favor of men, or black female counselors in favor of women. They may also accuse black counselors of being too uppity and bourgeois. When counselees cannot receive criticism and constantly transfer guilt to others, projection is the defense mechanism at work.

Minority counselees may employ affect and emotion as a means of resisting work. They will get angry with counselors or create an argument with spouses in the session to sabotage constructive therapeutic work. Some black women may cry as a method to avert responsibility.

The next way some counselees may avoid work is through the "we have tried that before" response to assigned prescriptions. They claim that the advice will not work and thus justify reasons why they should not spend time practicing it.

A final way that some African-American counselees resist working is by spiritualizing their inactivity. They usually make such statements as "The Lord showed me I shouldn't do that"; "That goes against my personal Christian belief"; "I don't feel led to do that"; "I need to pray about that first"; "I'll confer with my pastor and get back to you"; "I want to check that out in the Word." All seem like acceptable statements on the surface but may in fact be subtle ploys by Christian counselees to avoid working on their own problems. Counselors must be vigilant in identifying this sophistry.

Underlying these kinds of resistance are fear of change, fear of loss of power, anger, pride, and anxiety. These feelings must be exposed, the resistant behavior identified, and the inevitable consequences pointed out should lack of action continue. In a few cases counselors may exercise the threat to terminate therapy as a maneuver to elicit cooperation, but this works only when relationships are reasonably valued by counselees. Counselors may also contribute to blockage of the cooperative involving process. Counselors do not usually do this deliberately. Counselor blocks to cooperative involving take place inadvertently. Notwithstanding, it is every bit as problematic as counselee blocks. A case example will serve to show counselee blocks:

Ben and Harrah are a young Christian couple who came to counseling because of growing distance from each other and Ben's infidelity. The couple had been married for about seven years. I saw them three times. I had assigned them some communication-roles training to do at home, but at the session I detected resistance—the couple forgot their homework. Ben said he forgot to do his. Harrah's excuse was that Ben made her mad, so she didn't do her work. When I suggested that they work on it in the session, Harrah protested that it would not make any difference, since Ben did not really want to talk to her anyway. Harrah claimed she had been trying for the last few years to get Ben to talk to her, and he had not done it. I suggested they try anyway.

I requested that they move closer in the session, hold hands, and do the communication work. Ben was reluctant and at first refused. I pointed this out to him and encouraged his participation. As they went through the exercise they showed little effort. Several times Ben disrupted the process by not functioning correctly, refusing eye contact, going to the restroom, and asking for instructions to be repeated. I observed that the couple was very invested in maintaining their distance from each other. I asked the couple to stop the exercise, and I began processing what was going on. I pointed out that they were both resisting therapy and really did not seem motivated to work on their relationship. Harrah retorted that she had worked on her part for the last few months. I said that was not evident from the session with them. I suggested that I meet separately with them.

The individual sessions revealed that Ben was the oldest of three children. While growing up, he wanted to be close to his father, whom he loved very much. But Ben's father rejected him. Thus Ben resisted getting close to people for fear of being rejected.

Harrah, on the other hand, grew up in a family that had no boundaries. She felt engulfed by her family. Consequently, she did things to keep distance between herself and Ben for fear of being engulfed by him.

The couple had been operating on their respective family scripts. Once the dynamics had been shown them, they were more willing to work out their communication problems at the next session.

If counselees are willing to work with counselors, major changes can take place. If progress continues and the couple is mutually active in improving their relationship, they may expect success.

COUNSELOR BLOCKS TO COOPERATIVE INVOLVING

There are a number of ways that therapists and clergy may contribute to blocking cooperative involvement. The most obvious is simply not recognizing counselee blocks. If this occurs, counselors have been unwittingly enticed into the counselees' game.

Not so obvious is when counselors keep counselees dependent. Sometimes counselors work too hard trying to fulfill their own need to be needed. We counselors may volunteer to do things that counselees should be doing, like making phone calls that counselees are capable of making for themselves. In such cases we are working for, and no longer with, our counselees.

Not adequately preparing counselees for cooperative involvement is also a block to the process. Counselees will not perform what they do not know is their responsibility. Prior to the eunuch's baptism, Philip gave him the prerequisites for participation. Counselees need to be clear about what they have to do first, or they may be set up to fail.

NOTE

[1]Collins, 170–79.

17

POSITIVE TERMINATING

"The Spirit of the Lord caught away Philip, that the eunuch saw him no more" (Acts 8:39)

After Philip finished baptizing the eunuch, he had a remarkable divine experience. For when they came up out of the water "the Spirit of the Lord caught away Philip, that the eunuch saw him no more: and he went on his way rejoicing." Philip experienced optimum therapeutic termination!

Counseling must not be perpetual. There comes a time when counselors and counselees recognize that they have gone as far as they should go in the process, and that all good things must come to an end. Ending the counseling relationship correctly is as important as starting correctly. Termination of therapy is more than just saying good-bye; in Christian counseling it is also a benediction. The role of the Holy Spirit in the termination process as well as in preparing counselees are two areas warranting careful consideration by therapists.

THE ROLE OF THE HOLY SPIRIT IN TERMINATION

Philip's relationship with the Ethiopian was literally terminated by the Spirit of God. The dramatic way in which it happened suggests the primary role that the Holy Spirit has in this phase of counseling. We do not often know when or how to give closure to a relationship. We may feel the need to terminate a relationship with someone who should remain in therapy longer. Still, there may be other counselees who should stay in therapy but who in fact need to make a break from us.

Yielding to the Spirit in this phase means that we no longer have to rely solely on human judgment, but can draw from the very essence of God to make the decision. Not only that, but the possibility of error is now eliminated. Occasionally, as in the case of Philip, the Spirit will drastically remove us from a case, but not until God has been glorified, and counselee and counselor have been edified.

The Paraclete also assists us in preparing for termination. He is always present to help; we simply need to be more ready to receive that help.

PREPARING COUNSELEES FOR TERMINATION

In preparing counselees for termination, counselors need to perform a few key tasks. Encourage the counselee to review past performance and progress. In addition, work with counselees to determine further steps they need to take to insure continued growth.

At the end of the process, therapists may be less active in the interaction of a couple or individual. Counselees assume more and more responsibility for the counseling session. This phase must be followed by a session to discuss with counselees a termination date.

At the final session, some kind of closure is in order. A time of prayer and thanksgiving is an excellent way to close. An evaluative discussion may also be very rewarding for both parties.

Finally, counselors communicate best wishes, benedictions, and salutations to counselees, while indicating availability if they need continued assistance. After some time has elapsed, counselors should initiate follow-up contact to monitor the status of counselees. This is a supportive gesture in the estimation of many black clients.

The aim of Part Two has been to expound on ten biblical principles of the counseling process. Directive engaging, affecting joining, active listening, explorative questioning, correlative beginning, integrative witnessing, objective proceeding, effective counseling, cooperative involving, and positive terminating are biblical principles. Equipped with the awareness of issues that may confront them in therapy, and with the principles of developing and sustaining a successful process, counselors must know what intervention techniques to implement during the phase of therapy encompassing effective counseling.

Part III

COUNSELING INTERVENTIONS AND BLACK COUNSELEES

18

COUPLE AND INDIVIDUAL APPROACHES

The black family is experiencing a crisis. Fathers headed two-parent African-American households in the 1880s. As stated earlier, the 1880 census reported eighty-four percent of rural black families, and seventy-two percent of urban families, were two-parent households led by fathers. By 1986 forty-seven percent of black families were led by women. Though black women are less likely to marry, when they do their marriages are two times as likely to end in divorce. Some sociologists claim that at the root of the problem is the antipathy between black men and women.

Couple relationships must be a major focus of intervention. I differ with many black professionals in terms of the origin of the problem. Most of my colleagues point to racism and economics as causes of the trouble in black marriages. This is a very limited view because it does not explain why white couples, who occupy higher socioeconomic levels, experience many of the same problems. Nor does it take into account those black couples living at lower socioeconomic levels who enjoy harmonious marriages.

Racism and socioeconomics are two critical factors that influence black marriages. But racism and socioeconomics alone are ancillary to the real problem. Gary Collins states, "Marital problems are a deviation of Genesis 2:24."[1] The source of the problem remains our sinful nature expressed in rebellion against God's Word. Black men and women must return to the legacy of our ancestors who took their Christian religion seriously.

My counseling practice has shown a correlation between Christian faith and marital success. Part of clinical questioning includes an examination of a couple's involvement with the church and their belief in God. Couples with a strong religious orientation tend to stay in therapy longer and to improve significantly over those with a lightly held religious orientation.

This is consistent with the research done by Fulsinger and Wilson, who found that the greater the religious belief of the couple the higher the marital adjustment.[2] Pargament, Tyler, and Steele found in their study that individuals who attributed greater control to God concerning their lives manifested favorable psychosocial attributes.[3] These studies and my own experience suggest that Christian faith does benefit psychological dynamics as well as improve marital intervention with couples. Biblical marital counseling is a sound orientation for Christian counselors working with African-Americans.

BIBLICAL MARITAL COUNSELING WITH BLACK COUPLES

When counseling couples, counselors must be aware of themselves and of the special issues black couples bring to the sessions. Most couples come to therapy because of infidelity, the number one cause of black marital disruption. Usually it it the male who has been the offender, but the female may be involved. If the husband has been implicated in an extramarital relationship and has come to counseling with his wife, he will tend to be both reluctant to be there and defensive about the issue. If he is a Christian, he probably has strong defenses that serve to neutralize the conviction of the Holy Spirit. Counselors must focus on joining with him and confront him about his sin only after a trusting therapeutic relationship has developed. Counselors must approach the couple as a system in which both partners are contributors to the problem. Without this approach, counselors run the danger of forming a coalition with the woman and driving the black male out of therapy.

Therefore, counselors must help black wives acknowledge and confess their own culpability in their marital relationship.

Another common problem black couples will bring to counseling is economic problems. They frequently suffer from materialistic depression as they strive to climb the success ladder and encounter racism on virtually every rung. Arguments and conflicts in relation to their financial status are a common theme in these marriages. As mentioned earlier, black women may feel their husbands are overly frugal and financially irresponsible. Many black men think that their wives are covetous and extravagant spenders. Power-and-control conflicts follow, especially in dual-career couples.

Most problems for black professional women are caused by conflict between the demands of career and marriage.[4] Yet older black women decide that their marriages take precedence over their careers.[5] This may not be the case for younger black women. Problems around financial issues may appear more frequently among couples in their twenties and thirties. Christian counselors must help black couples deal with financial issues, and help them understand biblical principles concerning money matters.

A critical issue in bringing black couples to therapy is physical abuse. In most cases the woman is the victim. Counselors must stress the inconsistency of this behavior with Scripture; help abusers develop anger-reduction roles; enable couples to understand the different stages in the cycle of abuse; identify multigenerational patterns of abuse in family of origin; and teach couples better communication roles. I often use a nonviolence covenant between the couple and God—a promise of no physical assault. The idea of covenant has meaning for Christian black couples. But severe consequences (jail, disclosure to respected friends or employers, financial fines, etc.) must follow should the covenant be broken. If the woman is the victim, her physical safety is the priority. If there is danger to her, she should be removed from the house and both spouses should continue counseling separately.[6]

Enmeshment in the wider family also brings African-Americans to counseling. As mentioned earlier, black families tend to be fused intergenerationally. This may mean constant struggles with habits, attitudes, expectations and behavior stemming from their families of origin. Family-of-origin loyalties may be at odds with couple loyalties so that couples follow unhealthful family scripts in their relationships. The confusion of the past with the present is a prime cause of feelings of betrayal, accumulated resentments, and vicious attacks.

The two outstanding characteristics in problems with one's family of origin are nonselective repetition of the past and ignoring data available in the present.[7] Current marital problems may stem from attempts to master earlier family conflicts. Christian counselors enable couples to understand their family-of-origin messages, helping them break negative legacies, and become more differentiated through Christ and the power of the Spirit.

Another pattern in black couples is weak boundaries. They often have conflicts over distance versus closeness, inclusion and exclusion, lack of boundaries as a couple, and with extended families. Problems emerge from couples' inability to set and maintain boundaries for themselves and others. Counselors must help couples set boundaries and restructure interactive patterns.[8]

When couples bring problems with children to therapy, therapists make the marital interaction a part of the overall assessment. Problems around children reflect larger problems with couples. Counselors must support parents in regaining control where it has been relinquished; change those interactive patterns that provoke children to wrath; correct couples' distortions of biblical views on parenting; help couples set boundaries; promote their understanding of children's feelings and rights; restructure the family interaction to be consistent with Christian standards; encourage family devotion and leisure time; enable them to improve communication; exhort them to draw from extended-family strengths; be instrumental in increasing the overall sense of family self-esteem; and deal directly with couples' marital issues.

Understanding the kind of issues black couples bring to counseling will greatly enhance the success of interventions.

BIBLICAL THERAPEUTIC INTERVENTIONS

Therapeutic interventions are an important part of the counseling process. Most marital therapy approaches are appropriate, depending on the nature of the couple. Still, I recommend five approaches for use with black couples.

The first is the two-become-one approach. In Genesis we read, ". . . a man will leave his father and mother and be united to his wife, and they will become one flesh" (Genesis 2:24, NIV). This is one of the best pictures of a couple system. L'Abate describes a system as "a set of elements and rules that determine the relationships among the elements, and functions in a way that makes the whole greater than the sum of the two parts."[9] The whole of the one system is greater than two individuals. It is obvious from Genesis that God had a systems view. When using this approach, examine in what ways the two have become one. What is the nature of their system? How does it maintain homeostasis? In what manner do both of them encourage it? What are the rules and roles of the system? The aim is to find a suitable place to intervene, knowing that a change in one portion has effect on the whole system. Lest there be disastrous results, counselors must know how the couple system functions and what part they are changing. This approach is most useful with emeshed couples.

The second approach is the sins-of-the-fathers approach. It identifies the long-term negative familial interactions from one's family of origin. Exodus 20:5 says, "I punish the children for the sins of the fathers to the third and fourth generation" (NEB). Counselors look for negative features from the couple's family that have been generationally transmitted to present interactions. Counselors use genograms to collect family data, and encourage family visits when appropriate so that couples may work through unresolved issues with parents or other family members. Framo says that when adults are able to return and deal directly with their parents, brothers, and sisters about previously avoided issues, an opportunity exists for reconstructive changes to come about in their marital relationship.[10] Counselors instruct and motivate counselees to forgive their parents as Christ forgave them. In spite of what happened to counselees in the past, their steps were "ordered by the LORD" (Psalm 37:23). In Christ counselees can change their destiny and be liberated from their parents' sins. This method works favorably with African-American couples whose families are intergenerational by nature.

However, it is not without its limitations. Therapists must be able to differentiate the positive aspects of inherited patterns from negative. Counselors must be careful not to diagnose close familial ties as enmeshment. Strong family ties are a strength in black families.

Other difficulties with this approach arise when counselees are completely isolated from family. This makes it difficult to gather family data for genograms and engage other extended family members in therapy. It also increases resistance from couples in scheduling sessions with their parents. Nevertheless, if these challenges are met, a systems approach is a profitable intervention.

The third methodology implemented in therapy is the structure-of-the-household-of-God approach. This intervention is based on Ephesians 5:21–25, Colossians 3:18–21, and 1 Corinthians 11:3. God has an order and a structure for the home. When that order is changed, marital problems result. We have examined the fluidity endemic in the black family structure. Sometimes excessive fluidity results in frail or nonexistent boundaries. Moreover, fluid families often have an unbiblical power caste in which the children rule over the parents, the wife rules over the husband, or there is no clear authority figure in the home. Counselors facilitate the reordering of family hierarchy with therapeutic interventions such as restricting a domineering black woman's control in the session, giving a weak husband more time to talk; challenging the wife's position from a scriptural standpoint; teaching parents to establish limits with children who are out of control; or by assigning homework that rearranges the family's typical interaction.

With such couples counselors must emphasize their nonconformity to God's Word regarding marital polity. It is critical that the black woman affirm the biblical notion of the husband as head of the household. For a sizable group of black women, independence, dominance, and control have been a way of life.

They will not want to give this up easily. For these women, counselors must reframe the idea of submission as giving up an unbiblical role and not the diminishing of her power. As for the passive husband, counselors must gradually empower him to assume his role as head of the home. To accomplish this, counselors must model order and structure for the husband. Therapists must insist that the couple be present and punctual for sessions, and they must complete work assigned to them. Some black couples constantly assault boundaries set by counselors who show weakness.

The fourth intervention is the renewed-covenant approach. This technique is a synthesis of Clifford Sager's contracting theory and the biblical concept of covenant. Sager's theory is based on the assumption that couples come into marriage with interactional contracts that have a set of expectations, desires, wants, and wishes that are both conscious and unconscious. Each partner presumes the other will fulfill the expectations of his or her contract. If unfulfilled, marital tension increases.

Contracts fall into three categories of needs and expectations: expectations of marriage such as loyalty and support; intrapsychic and biological factors such as closeness and distance, dependence and independence; and lifestyle expectations.

Contracts have seven different marital-partner profiles: equal partners, who seek a relationship on equal terms; romantic partners, who are very possessive and hold their mates as sole objects of love and adoration; parental partners, who dominate their mates and make them childlike; childlike partners, who allow themselves to be dominated out of need for a parent; compassionate partners, who are companions to ward off loneliness; rational partners, who establish reasoned, logical, and well-ordered relationships; and parallel partners, who avoid intimacy and desire emotional distance.[11]

The final methodology to be discussed is the corrupt-communication approach from Ephesians 4:29. "Let no corrupt communication proceed out of your mouth, but that which is good to the use of edifying, that it may minister grace unto the hearers." In this approach, counselors highlight couples' unbiblical patterns of communication.

I have observed several communication styles with black Christian couples. The first is "Holy Ghosting." Spouses usurp the role of the Spirit, using tears, silence, moralizing, and self-righteous put-downs to make their mates feel guilty.

The second communication style is "false prophesying." This occurs when couples try to read the minds of their mates and forecast their feelings without letting mates speak for themselves. Usually the false prophet (the person forecasting) is wrong, but never learns.

Another style is "cursing." This style consists of negative labels spouses put on each other, often eliciting behavior that matches the label. It is further described in James 3:8–12.

The final communication style is "the double-mind bind." This happens when partners say one thing and do another, giving contradicting messages. The Scriptures say, "A double minded man is unstable in all his ways" (James 1:8). Such conduct makes for an unstable relationship.

Counselors must work with couples to improve their negative communication styles, and teach biblically based interaction. The approach used is behavioral. Therefore, to increase positive behavior, couples are encouraged to change their actions regardless of feelings.[12]

BIBLICAL INDIVIDUAL THERAPY

When doing individual therapy, three approaches are effective with African-American counselees.

The first approach is "as a man thinketh." This is a cognitive approach from Proverbs 23:7. Cognitive theory claims that it is what we tell ourselves about what is occurring that creates our feelings, behavior, and reactions. Black counselees come with many cognitive distortions about themselves, the world, and God. These distortions require loving confrontation. Wright suggests counselees must be helped to see that what they think determines their view of a situation. Counselors must help counselees become observers of their thoughts and make positive statements contrary to negative thoughts and behavior. Finally, counselors need to help them to take steps that make the new changes permanent.[13] Generally, counselors should focus on cognitive distortions related to negative self-esteem or powerlessness, and utilize the Scriptures to correct distortions.

The second approach is multigenerational ("sins of the fathers"). Counselors go over family-of-origin issues that relate to counselees' problems, and urge extended family sessions where possible. This approach parallels that used with couples.

Finally, the "Christian-conduct" behavioral approach is employed with blacks whose behavioral problems are based in anxiety. Treatment involves focusing on positive behavior and increasing such behavior while decreasing negative ones. Using the Bible to praise counselees and raise their self-esteem is of great benefit in this method. Whether counselors are working with couples or individuals, if they desire to be a conduit for God's grace, power, and wisdom, they will enable their brothers' and sisters' development in the kingdom of God and their conformity to the image of Jesus Christ.

CONCLUSION

The aim of this section has been to expound on ten biblical principles of the counseling process. I have shown that directive engaging, affective joining, active listening, explorative questioning, correlative beginning, integrative witnessing, objective proceeding, effective counseling, cooperative involving, and positive terminating are biblical principles. They are derived from Acts 8:26–39. Equipped with the awareness of the issues that may confront them in sustaining a successful counseling process, therapists and clergy must know what therapeutic intervention techniques to implement for effective counseling.

NOTES

[1]Collins, 170–79.

[2]Erik E. Filsinger and Margaret R. Wilson, "Religiosity, Socio-economic Rewards and Family Development: Predictors of Marital Adjustment," *Journal of Marriage and the Family* (August 1984): 68.

[3]Kenneth I. Pargament, Forrest B. Tyler, and Robert E. Steele, *God Control, Personal Control and Individual Psychosocial Effectiveness* (Univ. of Maryland, 1986), 1.

[4]Cheryl B. Leggon, "Career, Marriage, and Motherhood: Coping Out or Coping In," *Black Marriage and Family Therapy*, ed. Constance E. Obudho, (Westport: Greenwood, 1983), 133.

[5]Ibid., 169.

[6]Robert W. Beavers, *Successful Marriage: A Family Systems Approach to Couple Therapy* (New York: W. W. Norton, 1985), 61.

[7]James L. Framo, "The Integration of Marital Therapy With Sessions With Family of Origin," *Handbook of Family Therapy* (New York: W. W. Norton, 1985), 61.

[8]Salvador Minuchin and Charles H. Fishman, *Family Therapy Techniques* (Cambridge: Harvard Univ. Press, 1981), 144–46.

[9]L'Abate, 244.

[10]Framo, 134.

[11]Clifford J. Sager and Bernice Hunt, *Intimate Partners: Hidden Patterns in Love Relationships* (New York: McGraw-Hill), 12–26.

[12]Wright, 125.

[13]Ibid.

CONCLUSION

It has been our aim to share the biblical principles and clinical approaches we have found successful in practice with black clients in Christian marital therapy. We selected methodologies from case experience with anecdotal examples. We stated at the outset our awareness of the insufficiencies and limits of such an approach in terms of scientific rigor.

By the same token we have sought to present the clinical approach as a kind of research that emerges from the clinician's experience and observations. It is our belief that the clinical approach somewhat maligned by counselors in secular mental health professions can be endorsed by Christian counselors. The Bible that we revere and defend so tenaciously is the recording by God's clinicians—the prophets, apostles, and other godly people—of the observed interactions of God with his creatures and his creatures' interactions with each other.

Moreover, we have sought to relay seven issues blacks bring to therapy that affect the clinical process, including ethnicity, gender, sexual identity, power, socio-economics, environment, and religion. We have discussed ten principles—directive engaging, affective joining, active listening, explorative questioning, correlative beginning, integrative witnessing, objective proceeding, effective counseling, cooperative involving, and positive terminating—as significant elements of an effective clinical process. We have shared the enlightenment received from Acts 8:26–39 concerning how a black person from Ethiopia had a cognitive as well as a spiritual problem resolved by the use of these principles. Finally, we have tried to show how those same principles are relevant to Christian counseling with African-Americans today.

We understand the need for more statistical data and research by evangelicals with respect to the Christian religion and African-American people. But we also believe that the mere experience of observing the "Ethiopian's chariot," doing scales and surveys about the Ethiopian and his chariot, is not the same as riding in the chariot. The clinician understands the joy of the ride and the honor of being invited by the Ethiopian to come up and sit.

God has allowed me to ride in the chariots of many black people, not only with them but as one of them. What I have learned is that the Christian counselor who wants to counsel black clients from a biblical perspective—who is willing to make himself available to the Holy Spirit, who wants to show the love of God to people who have been oppressed, who is committed to the Bible as the final authority on counseling, and who will carefully consider the issues and principles expounded in this book—is an excellent prospect for a most interesting ride in the Ethiopian's chariot.

BIBLIOGRAPHY

Banks, William L. *The Black Church in the U.S.: Its Origin, Growth, Contribution and Outlook.* Chicago: Moody, 1972.

Barnard, Charles P., and Ramon Garrido Corrales. *The Theory and Technique of Family Therapy.* Springfield: Bannerstone House, 1979.

Beavers, W. Robert. *Successful Marriage: A Family Systems Approach to Couples Therapy.* New York: W. W. Norton, 1985.

Brooke, John D. *The Five Major Doctrines of the Christian Faith.* Newburgh, Ind.: Brooke Ministries, 1982.

Collins, Gary R. *Christian Counseling: A Comprehensive Guide.* Waco: Word, 1980.

Crabb, Lawrence J. *Effective Biblical Counseling: A Model for Helping Caring Christians Become Capable Counselors.* Grand Rapids: Zondervan, 1977.

Davis, George, and Jill Nelson. "Come Out With Your Hands: How Black Men and Women Really Feel About Each Other." *Essence.* (July 1986): 54–56.

Dobson, James. *What Wives Wish Their Husbands Knew About Women.* Wheaton: Tyndale, 1975.

Filisinger, Erik E., and Margaret R. Wilson. "Religiosity, Socioeconomic Rewards and Family Development: Predictors of Marital Adjustment." *Journal of Marriage and the Family.* (August 1984): 663–69.

Friedman, Edwin H. *Generation to Generation: Family Process in Church and Synagogue.* New York: Guilford Press, 1985.

Gilder, George F. *Sexual Suicide.* New York: Bantam Books, 1975.

Gray-Little, Bernadette. "Marital Quality and Power Processes Among Black Couples." *Journal of Marriage and the Family* (August 1982): 633–44.

Grier, William H., and Price M. Cobbs. *Black Rage.* New York: Basic Books, 1968.

————. *The Jesus Bag.* New York: Basic Books, 1971.

Griffith, James L. "Employing the God-Family Relationship in Therapy With Religious Families." *Family Process* 25 (December 1986): 609–18.

Guldseth, G. J. *Emotional Ills and the Christian.* Plainfield: Logos, 1969.

Gurman, Alan S., and David P. Kniskern, eds. *Handbook of Family Therapy.* New York: Brunner/Mazel, 1981.

Gutman, Herbert H. *The Black Family in Slavery and Freedom 1750–1915*. New York: Vintage Books, 1976.

Huggins, Nathan. *Black Odyssey: The Afro-American Ordeal in Slavery*. New York: Random House, 1977.

Hyder, Quentin Q. *The Christian's Handbook of Psychiatry*. Old Tappan: Spire Books, 1973.

Korchin, Sheldon J. "Clinical Psychology and Minority Problems." *American Psychologist* (March 1980): 262–69.

L'Abate, Luciano, and Bess L'Abate. *How To Avoid Divorce: Help for Troubled Marriages*. Atlanta: John Knox, 1977.

L'Abate, Luciano, Gary Ganahl, and James C. Hanien. *Methods of Family Therapy*. Englewood: Prentice-Hall, 1986.

McAdoo, Harriette Pipes, ed. *Black Families*. Beverly Hills: Sage Publications, 1981.

Meier, Paul D., Frank B. Minirth, and Frank B. Wichern. *Introduction to Psychology and Counseling: Christian Perspectives and Application*. Grand Rapids: Baker, 1982.

Miles, Herbert J. *Sexual Happiness in Marriage: A Christian Interpretation of Sexual Adjustment in Marriage*. Grand Rapids: Zondervan, 1972.

Minuchin, Salvador, and Charles H. Fishman. *Family Therapy Technique*. Cambridge: Harvard Univ. Press, 1981.

Narramore, Bruce M. *No Condemnation: Rethinking Guilt Motivation in Counseling, Preaching, and Parenting*. Grand Rapids: Zondervan, 1984.

_____. *Psychology of Counseling*. Grand Rapids: Zondervan, 1968.

Norment, Lynn. "The Truth About AIDS." *Ebony* (April 1987): 126–28.

Obudho, Constance E., ed. *Marriage And Family Therapy*. Westport: Greenwood, 1983.

Osborne, Cecil G. *Understanding Your Past, The Key to the Future*. Waco: Word, 1980.

Pargament, Kenneth I., Forrest B. Tyler, and Robert E. Steele. *God Control, Personal Control and Individual Psychosocial Effectiveness*. Univ. of Maryland, 1986.

Pearce, John K., and Monica McGoldrick, eds. *Ethnicity And Family Therapy*. New York: Guildford, 1982.

Poissant, Alvin. *Why Blacks Kill Blacks*. New York: Emerson Hall, 1972.

Sager, Clifford J., and Bernice Hunt. *Intimate Partners: Hidden Patterns in Love Relationships*. New York: McGraw-Hill, 1979.

Scanzoni, John H. *The Black Family in Modern Society*. Boston: Allynard Bacon, 1971.

_____. *Sexual Bargaining: Power Politics in American Marriage*. Englewood Cliffs: Prentice-Hall, 1972.

Staples, Robert. *Black Masculinity: The Black Males' Role in American Society*. San Francisco: Black Scholar Press, 1982.

Taylor, Robert Joseph. "Receipt of Support From Family Among Black Americans and Familial Differences." *Journal of Marriage and the Family* 48 (February 1986), 67–77.

Tournier, Paul. *To Understand Each Other*. Atlanta: John Knox, 1974.

Weeks, Gerald R., and Larry Hof, eds. *Integrating Sex and Marital Therapy: A Clinical Guide*. New York: Brunner-Mazel, 1987.

Wright, H. Norman. *Marital Counseling a Biblical Cognitive Approach*. New York: Harper and Row, 1981.

INDEX OF PERSONS

SCRIPTURE INDEX

Acts 8 is not included in the index because of its frequent reference owing to the thematic structure of this book.